EDUCATING FOR DIVERSITY

EDUCATING
FOR DIVERSITY

Betty Atwell *Stebbins* Wright, *1919-*
[*Elizabeth*]

ILLUSTRATED

THE JOHN DAY COMPANY

NEW YORK

The photographs in this book are reproduced by courtesy of the following organizations and photographers:

American Friends Service Committee:
  1 (photograph by Paul S. Buck), 2, 3 (by Phiz), 4, 7, 12 (by Paul S. Buck)

Reginald Jackson, New Haven, Connecticut:
  5, 8, 10

New Haven Register:
  6 (photograph by Art Dietle)

New York State Department of Education:
  9 (photograph by David Brooks)

United Nations:
  11

CONTENTS

5

Illustrations will be found following page 96.

FOREWORD AND
ACKNOWLEDGMENTS

Diversity means difference: change, variety, and multiformity. It also means educating for uncertainties that are increasingly part of living today, and for a better world than the one we know or have known. These times have directed our attention to the demands and needs of poverty-stricken and disadvantaged families, the growth of urbanization, and rapid technological changes. But there are children growing up in families and neighborhoods of the well-to-do where there are merciless pressures for homogeneity, conformity, and achievement. Such children are as much in need of education that has meaning and diversity as are the deprived. There are many factors that get in the way of human potentiality and productive citizenship.

This book is about the kinds of community-school support needed for education that will advance dignity, equal opportunity, full citizenship, and selfhood in a diverse, precarious, and changing world. Although these principles underlie our prevailing ethics and are cherished as the most basic social policies and doctrines of this country, many groups of citizens have never yet enjoyed this heritage. The American dream of equality and hope for oneself and one's children can still be realized through our system of public education. With concerted effort, it is possible for youngsters of all ethnic groups, heritages, and social circumstances to be brought into the mainstream of American life and to identify with full citizenship and with programs advanced under the aegis of communities through their public schools.

As we face the tasks of providing quality education and equality of educational opportunity for all children, and as schools struggle with problems of embeddedness and tradition, financing education for ever-growing numbers of students, implementing new grouping patterns, and creating new materials and techniques, each of us can gain a new sense of belonging—of investment in life and humanity—and of regeneration through democracy. The challenges are unequaled in American life to date, but our responsibilities are quite clear.

Education for equal opportunity is not the job of the schools alone, but becomes the responsibility of the total social complex that involves community agencies, teachers' colleges, universities, public school policy-makers and educators, and every citizen. Without total coordinated interaction and concern, public schools can never hope to fulfill the roles for which they were intended and they may cease to exist at all. If, however, they do continue to exist, they must finally accept the challenge of educating multiethnic, multiracial, and socially diverse American citizens to their fullest potentiality. Although the idea of separation developed early in the history of public education, it has persisted too long. The premise that there can be "separate but equal" educational opportunity has proven to be false with the growing recognition of the need for educating for diversity.

Each of us is made up, in a large part at least, of the other lives that have touched and influenced our own. There are many people I should like to mention here whose philosophies, commitments, and actions have become an integral part of mine, and who are thus present in the pages of this book. They have been teachers, colleagues, and friends who have possessed the kind of humanity, courage, and openness that reach out to affect the lives of all who have known them. It is impossible to mention them all but among them are: E. Lewis B. Curtis, recently retired Professor of History of State University College, Oneonta, New York, and now teaching on the island of Guam; the late Samuel Mclaughlin, Professor of Educational Supervision at New York University and Dean of the School of Education at the University of Utah; Laurence G. Paquin, Superintendent of Baltimore, Maryland, Public Schools, and former Superintendent of New Haven Public Schools, New Haven, Connecticut; Ethel Alpenfels, Professor of Anthropology at New York University; Aileen Robinson, formerly with the Public Schools of Scarsdale, New York, and now Director of the American Community School in Beirut, Lebanon; Betty Warner Dietz, a former teaching colleague and now Professor of Education at Brooklyn College; and Dan Dodson, Director of the Center for Human Relations and Community Studies at New York University, and coordinator of the Inservice Intergroup Education seminars in New Haven, Connecticut.

I dedicate this book to my mother, whose love, faith, and devotion to her family and to all who have known her have been a constant inspiration and demonstration. Her courage, humanity, and compassion have influenced many people beyond the hills and valleys of our tiny upstate New York village, and her faith and constant encouragement have endured through unremitting hardships and adversities. From her, my brothers and I first learned that one must educate oneself for life's diversities and that such education helps one respond productively to life's new encounters.

BETTY ATWELL WRIGHT

EDUCATING FOR DIVERSITY

CHAPTER 1

CRITICAL ISSUES IN THE SIXTIES

DIVERSITY in this century has not only produced the biggest revo-
lutions in all of human history, but has also given rise to the
worst wars and the worst depressions. And *diversity* in the
twentieth century has worn many faces. Among these are the
contrasting faces of plenty and of poverty—of love and of hate—
of fear and of courage—of despair and of hope—of agrarian pasts
and of urban futures—of provincialism and of social change.

Schools and the social milieus they represent have often chosen
to ignore the values of diversity in American life. Traditional
citizenship and human relations courses and committees have done
little to change the attitudes or actions of a prominent Alabama
citizen who recently said, "Repugnant as it is to us, we had better
comply with the law," or the teacher who said, "They're all right
in their own place, but I don't want them in my class," or the
teen-age self-styled "Klansmen" in Connecticut and elsewhere
who have been burning crosses and otherwise threatening and
harassing Negro, Portuguese, and Puerto Rican families because
their groups advocate White supremacy.

The challenge to America, and especially to schools in this
country, is a redefinition of the role of education in intergroup
relations during these times of social change and conflict. After

the elimination of segregated schools, there are many other things to do, since intragroup and intergroup tensions and misunderstandings can still defeat democracy. We must move immediately to initiate plans for eliminating *de facto* segregation in communities and in schools; build bridges too long missing between the streets and the schools; eliminate the tragic divorces between living and learning; permeate regular curriculum subjects with methods and materials for intercultural understanding, and value heterogeneity above homogeneity.

We have not been totally unsuccessful, for some of our young people express their beliefs about what lies ahead and what they intend to do about the future. One young female college student who has been participating in social action groups and tutorial programs for neighborhood children believes that people must "listen, learn, be moved, participate, and not be afraid to change. It makes me sad," she continues, "to see those who once worked enthusiastically for their ideals but who no longer see any reason why they should do so. This is what has happened to our parents and it is my hope that it will not happen to us. My friends and I want to help change the world and we believe that together we can."

Another young man, a college senior about to enter the Peace Corps, states his convictions this way: "This generation is trying to redefine its humanity. Some college students are *acting* on their social convictions rather than just exchanging intellectual platitudes as many before them have done. We want a new humanism. Past generations have been too unwilling to commit themselves—to *move to the action level.* This new generation is trying to develop a total social consciousness—they *go to Mississippi* instead of just talking about it."

Young people like these give the world renewed hope that old conflicts of purposes, goals, values, and satisfactions may be resolved through education for action that will move civilization from the myths and images of rural societal pasts to the new urban society which is in evolution and has not yet achieved a definite shape or form. Some Americans still live and work in parts of the country where religious, racial, socioeconomic, and ethnic differences are minimal or ignored. Many thousands of others live and work in urban complexes where they are experiencing changes they cannot afford to ignore.

Among a citizenry that was to have benefited from public education for "citizenship" and better "human relations," there are familiar old cleavages and hatreds being perpetuated. New upheavals represent mankind's stubborn search for self-identity and opportunity for citizenry that will grant human rights to last century's slaves. Previous generations have left a legacy of dilemmas and dichotomies. But this generation has a responsibility to leave a better legacy for future generations.

Within this century, how many children have grown to warped adulthood because of prejudice and social, class, and color distinction? How many have never yet enjoyed the benefits of democracy and the opportunity to pursue "life, liberty, and happiness" because of the color of their skin, the temple at which they worship, or the place where they live? How many died in gas chambers and slave labor camps so that society could operate unhampered by divergent views? How many existed in hopeless and helpless isolation without the benefit of decent education, job and housing opportunities, or adequate health and medical services?

None of these problems is really new. But today they are set in a new context. This year in the United States there are over forty-one million children who are ten years of age or under. This is more than the entire population of the country one hundred years ago. Yet in many respects, segments of our society and the schools that represent it are operated with the attitudes and actions of the last century's horse-and-buggy era. Old recipes cannot work well in these times. New elements are needed to meet the educational demands of the space age. The questions we must ask today are open-ended—they have no pat answers; they inevitably lead to other questions and many possible recommendations and solutions. If we look to public schools for leadership, we must do more than offer lip service to "quality" education.

Teachers' colleges, community policy-makers, public school administrators, and teachers are reexamining many assumptions and current practices in the selection of teachers and the kind of education they receive, school financing and site selection, school organization, and curriculum innovation, as they investigate ways of freeing human resources for the benefit of society. These critical reevaluations require facing pertinent facts and conditions so that those charged with the responsibility may act decisively, creatively, and dynamically in an age when seventy percent of the world's population is living in or near cities.

Neighborhood and New Migrant Dilemmas

The history of cities and suburbs in the United States shows a progression of movement from rural to urban areas, from southern to northern parts of the country, and from neighborhood to neighborhood, as new groups arrive and older groups move to suburbia, resulting in different kinds of choices regarding living, educating, working, and utilizing leisure time. The decisions will determine whether ours is to be a decadent or a dynamic future.

In the past and present, each new group has inherited the heart of the city but, because of economic conditions, has been relegated to certain neighborhoods. As fortunes improved, each group moved "out and up" to make way for the next groups. Unskilled labor was still in great demand, and those trained for a special skill or profession found ready markets for their talents. Old-timers resented newcomers, and people tended to entrench in new neighborhoods by ethnic group and social class. The first "different" families to move into old neighborhoods were discouraged or ignored, but in the absence of color differences, they eventually learned to function in comparative harmony. Early groups, although vindictive and resentful without understanding why, did not bomb one another's homes and churches, kill one another's children, or try to prevent one another from gaining full citizenship privileges. Their methods of gaining status were often questionable and even illegal, but there was some kind of employment for all. History is replete with examples of school quotas for certain ethnic groups, but these have been gradually eliminated through social pressures and action. Earlier waves of migrants were identifiable by country of origin, ethnic group characteristics that they wished to retain, language, and religious preferences. For these groups there was a certain security in their heritage, even though they faced many other difficulties as newcomers.

Today, the newest migrant groups to cities, especially to northern cities, are more identifiable by color than by the multiple characteristics of earlier groups. They have inherited a history of degradation and torture in a country they did not choose but *to which they were brought and sold into slavery*. They were denuded of names, all personal rights, and even family membership. It was once illegal to teach them to read; theirs have been the most menial job opportunities, the most inadequate housing and schooling, and the denial of a cultural and ethnic heritage of which they could be proud. The "affluent society" and the "land of golden opportunity" have not been for them. Old prejudices and hatreds have driven them from the states of their birth to new areas with the hope that life can yet be fulfilled for them. Unfortunately they have inherited the ghettos in the decadent hearts of cities that have been vacated by preceding generations of newcomers.

The Negro Americans arriving in cities today, uprooted from familiar surroundings and unprepared by education or experience for the complexities of urban life and modern living, are finding that willing hearts and strong bodies are not enough. All

of the old hatreds and stereotyping return to haunt them in the
new situation, perpetuated by the very ones who, only a generation or two ago, were subjected to the same kind of treatment
because they were "different." A later chapter will be devoted to
the nature of prejudice and stereotyping, but here it will suffice
to say that there is no such thing as one Negro culture, Negro
language, or Negro characteristic for the Negro-American group
as a whole to fall back on as have groups of previous newcomers.
Yet these new migrants have been American pioneers and citizens
for longer periods of time than many of their fellow citizens who
have become assimilated. The Negro American's heritage has
been continued human bondage and exploitation.

In pioneering efforts to open new doors of opportunity and
create new kinds of interpersonal associations for people of
minority groups, some cities are boldly attacking the problems
of *de facto* segregation and cultural deprivation by community-
sponsored public integrated housing; redevelopment and re-
location projects; and retraining and adult education projects.
Concentrated attention is being given to problems of juvenile delinquency, school dropouts, and equal opportunities in education,
employment, and housing. These programs can make a real difference for many people, but in the absence of total commitment
to the necessity for them, they are too few and far between.

In the schools, we have hopefully assumed that the most vital
importance of our work had to do with improving attitudes and
educational opportunities for young people. But too often we
have found ourselves *following the leaders* rather than *setting the
pace*. Newspaper headlines in any city will attest all too eloquently
to the ridicule, character assassination, and threats to which public
officials who propose necessary changes are subjected.

There are also instances where boards of education and school
superintendents who take dynamic leadership in redistricting and
redistribution plans are castigated by groups who consider the old
neighborhoods and the old ways sacrosanct. Plans that involve

"racial balance," "quality education for all," "interethnic group-ing," "school pairing," relocated educational parks, and pupil-teacher population shifts have acted as catalysts for violent feel-ings, actions, and recriminations. Bond issues for support of public education are defeated; waiting lists of private and parochial schools grow longer; those who can afford to, move to the sub-urbs; funds are withheld; the public blindly demands new school superintendents and new school boards; court cases pile up; poli-ticians make political heydays during the chaos; and everyone with an axe to grind gets into the act. It is no wonder that some educators *know* better than they *do*.

These negative attitudes and delaying tactics neither bode well for the future of public education, especially in cities, nor do they create conditions that can effect the *action* necessary to cure the ills of our society. Intergroup education cannot take place in the segregated schools and neighborhoods of the past. The neighbor-hood-school concept is undergoing close scrutiny, as well it should, but the neighborhood dilemma remains, and so does the lack of equal opportunity for millions of new migrants. Municipalities must look for new ways to educate and new sources of revenue to support more effective education for today's urban millions. Added to these responsibilities is the need to exercise leadership in helping citizens develop a social conscience that will encourage them to become more involved in new encounters and confronta-tions.

Academic Pressures and Grouping Problems

Neighborhood and new-migrant dilemmas have come at a time when schools are more pressured than ever before for academic excellence. The Sputnik era catapulted local, state, and national demands for achievements unprecedented in any other era of our history. Thus we inherit existing and new social problems while facing increased demands for scholarship. With these pressures for scholarship, and increased demands for tightening up the curriculum all down the line from college to kindergarten, we are sometimes forced into segregating groups of students who have been advantaged over a longer period of time from those that have been educationally deprived. Even teachers react to these pressures by demanding more homogeneous grouping, more "special" teachers for the educationally disadvantaged, and more "tracks" for school placement.

Under such circumstances, it is difficult to create any prolonged intergroup contacts, even during lunch hours and gymnasium periods, because of tightened scheduling and increased regulation. We must ask ourselves whether the goals of scholarship and the goals of citizenship can be made compatible. Since reflection on this point reveals that they are really inseparable, then action is needed that will lead us toward more upward mobility for all students and greater opportunity for longer periods of contact and achievement in an atmosphere based upon the recognition that talents vary and that variety of personal contacts can result in social acceptance and intellectual competence.

De facto segregation exists *in neighborhoods and therefore in neighborhood schools*. Society certainly tends to see segregated and homogeneous schools as inferior. We have ample proof, too, that children from overcrowded, underprivileged, culturally deprived, and segregated homes and neighborhoods learn at an early age from one another that life is not promising—that aspirations are either nonexistent or to no avail. We have been increasingly unwilling or unable to accept the fact that young people have been learning far more from others like them on the streets and in their neighborhoods than they have learned in schools. Teachers wonder why the things they *think* they have taught have not been learned, but they continue teaching the literature of other centuries, the classics of another era, language usage that dates from the Latin Grammar School days, history courses that accentuate dates and memorization rather than cause and effect with present-day applications, and lecture-drill courses *ad infini-*

tum. Schools fail to look for imaginative new ways to teach, ways to bridge the gaps between living and learning, and ways to group and regroup so that scholarship *and* citizenship can function simultaneously.

The "Myth of Homogeneity"[1] may have colored the thinking of citizens and citizen-teachers for so long that they tend to see children in homogeneous groups—in homogeneous neighborhoods, with homogeneous families—pigeonholed by number, kind, achievement, aspiration, and culture-based IQ tests. It is time to stop giving *lip service* to phrases such as quality education for all, value of heterogeneity in society, individual differences, and show through *action* that all youngsters are potentially creative, potentially productive, and potentially valuable human beings.

Since the real job of education is to take each child where he is and help him go as far as he can, and since real homogeneity is neither possible nor advisable, we need to look very carefully at any practice that involves either homogeneous neighborhood or homogeneous class grouping. Do not educators *talk* about individual differences, individualized and personalized instruction, and allowing each student to develop his own greatest potential, while continuing to put every child through the same book in the same way at the same time as they react to pressures for more homogeneous groups? Do we not insist that conformity and "alikeness" be taught as a way of life through the practices and techniques being used in too many of today's schools? There has been a mounting body of research for the past thirty years which shows that students grouped by likenesses tend to become more alike, tend to support the negative aspects of the "group," and tend to see themselves as they think others see them.

Further, there is no research that indicates that the high achiever is penalized by being with those less gifted than he, or that IQ or achievement are either constant or accurately measur-

[1] Don Dodson, "Intergroup Relations" lectures, New Haven, Conn. (Inservice Intergroup Education All-Staff Project, New Haven Bd. of Ed.), 1964.

able factors. Yet some children learn *failure as a way of life* from first grade on in schools because they are relegated to a group with so-called similar needs; in other words, they are grouped with those supposedly *like* them. Fortunately, in those places where different combinations have taken place and where schools have broken with tradition, we are beginning to accumulate evidence that poorly motivated, environmentally deprived children benefit through being with students who are more highly motivated and have different aspirations. It seems fair to assume that there are immeasurable benefits for privileged and gifted learners in learning to live with and work with others of varied talents and accomplishments.

Self-Concept Research

In a study made of the self-concepts of 102 fifth-graders grouped according to ability and taught separately beginning with the first grade, Maxine Mann in discussing "Ability Grouping"[2] reported:

In the *top section,* twenty-five children gave positive responses in terms of ability or achievement—twenty-one in *positive* "I" terms. *No negative* responses were made.

In the *next lower section,* Section Two, there were *only seven* responses in terms of ability or achievement; and in *Section Three only five.*

In Section Four, *the lowest,* the fourteen responding in terms of ability or achievement *gave negative responses*—six in "I" terms, seven in "we" terms. It is interesting to note that there are *no negative responses* in Sections One and Two, few in Section Three, and *only negative responses* in Section Four.

In another research study reported by Miriam Goldberg[3] on

[2] Maxine Mann, "What Does Ability Grouping Do to the Self-Concept?" *Childhood Education,* April 1960, pp. 357–61, ACEI, Washington, D.C.
[3] Miriam L. Goldberg, "Studies in Underachievers Among Academically Talented," *Freeing Capacity to Learn,* 1960, p. 58, ASCD, Washington, D.C.

the basis of studies in underachievement of the academically talented, she says:

. . . the underachiever perceives himself as less able to fulfill the tasks required of him, less eager to learn, less confident in himself, and less ambitious.

Much of the evidence in such studies seems to negate the feasibility of grouping children according to ability, and implies that ability grouping may contribute to undesirable attitudes and self-concepts, especially among those who are classified as "slow learners," "late bloomers," and "underachievers."

The August 2, 1959, *New York Times* reported a study by David A. Abramson of the New York City Research Bureau:

The study followed high-school graduates through their freshman and sophomore years in college . . . the report showed that there were no statistically significant differences observed in any instance in the grade-point averages earned by students who had been members of organized ability groups in their respective high schools and students who had not been grouped on an ability basis!

The problem of how to group students, like other current educational and social dilemmas, raises more questions than it answers. But it does highlight the general lack of public knowledge about the research that has existed for a long time but has never reached school practice. It also emphasizes the fact that current pressures on the part of lay people and educators for more homogeneous grouping is simply returning to past practices rather than pushing ahead to new frontiers.

For further annotated studies and conclusions, review the findings of research studies in grouping that have been conducted and reported. The entire question of grouping would undergo drastic revision in updated behaviors and action if the research that exists were translated into new action models.

A valuable resource for those interested in grouping practices is a pamphlet called "Toward Effective Grouping,"[4] published by the Association for Childhood Education International. In the article "The Grouping Question—1930–1962," Dr. Alice V. Keliher reports research conclusions reached in 1931 and parallels them with more recent studies by scholars in the intervening years.[5] A sample from this report follows:

1930 Conclusions: Keliher	*Subsequent Findings*[6]
Children do discern the reasons for their segregation into groups and attribute their placement in most cases to a "general level" of ability. This is a harmful concept, for the individual's supposition that it does exist is likely to cause him to neglect, repress or remain in ignorance of abilities which are not called out in the routine of an academic school day. The differentiation of curricula may easily lead to the fixing of environmental conditions which, in turn, may fix possibilities of development for the child.	Not only later educational opportunities but subsequent job opportunities become increasingly fixed by earlier school performance. The late bloomer, the early rebel, the child from an educationally different home—all of them, in full scale meritocracy, become victims of an often senseless irreversibility of decision.

Therefore, we must ask ourselves why we group as we do, and whether schools as they exist are basing their practices on valid assumptions about grouping and possible teaching-learning experiences. Are teachers partially responsible for stereotyping children when they insist upon tighter academic grouping? Do outmoded curricula hamper more defensible grouping practices? Can educators use the technology at their command to make self-study and self-progress possible for some students in some curricu-

---

[4] ACEI, "Toward Effective Grouping," Washington, D.C., pp. 1–56, 75¢.
[5] Alice V. Keliher, "A Critical Study of Homogeneous Grouping," TC Bureau of Publication, Columbia U., Contribution to Education, #452.
[6] Jerome S. Bruner, *The Process of Education* (Cambridge, Harvard University Press), p. 77.

lar areas? Can any school or any community defend homogeneous grouping while it attempts to find modern ways to teach the humanities, social sciences, and the art of communication among many kinds of students? Do schools make the right assumptions about the climate in which students can relate to one another and enrich one another's lives? Does education as it presently exists relegate some children to a life of failure, to menial and unimportant tasks, to enforced leisure because they are unemployable, to early school dropout, and to lower image of self, by making premature and often invalid judgments about them? These are among the questions the twentieth century raises, and these are the questions which must be answered through inculcated attitudes, substantial effort, and knowledgeable innovations.

Assumptions About Children

Assumptions about grouping are inescapably linked to assumptions about human potentialities and about children. Out of one side of our mouths we say, "As the twig is bent . . . ," believing that teaching *can* make an important difference for every child. But out of the other side of our mouths we are too prone to say, "Well—like father, like son, you know," as though education and environment make no difference anyway. Are there certain kinds of children from certain kinds of families and neighborhoods from whom little or nothing is expected? There are! It is demoralizing to hear teachers in many schools apologize for what they *haven't* been able to do. Increasingly they excuse indifferent teaching with comments such as "I have the slow (or low) ones, you know," "Well, these children are from *that* neighborhood," or "Well, what can you expect from these kinds of children?" Is the problem really in human potentiality, or in the myths and perceptions of society and the schools that represent it?

Just as children who are grouped by so-called *kinds of problems* tend to give one another negative support and produce few leaders of the positive sort, so, too, when we expect less of children, we tend to demand less of them. They, in turn, *tend to become less*. At a time when larger segments of our population than ever before require improved self-images, models of inspiration, "possiblism," and increased opportunities, there is unprecedented opportunity to provide these needs. Do your community and your schools answer these challenges?

There are some pilot projects financed by both private foundations and federal funds that give promise of lifting ceilings for all children. Among them are programs such as prekindergarten classes, summer schools, Higher Horizons projects, youth mobilization, work-study programs, and after-school tutoring. These programs are sprinkled about great cities where millions dwell in slums, but as yet they touch too few children who could be benefited. One reason may be that as funds are withdrawn after initial grants, local schools are sometimes unable and often unwilling to pick up the tab for financing them and incorporating them into regular school budgets and programs. Some community leaders even attack them as "socialistic experiments" that will go away if they are ignored or attacked. The conditions that necessitate them will *not* go away unless a concerted attack is continued on a much broader basis at the source of the problem. *Later will be too late.*

This country cannot afford one day, one week, or one year of wasting its most valuable natural resource—*human potential.* Somehow the human and financial resources must be found with which to extend the school day, the school year, and the educational programs that are centered in schools and communities. This must be done before another generation of uneducated and unemployable persons is added to the relief rosters. Relief and unemployment doles dissipate funds in ways that contribute to neither the dignity nor the rights of citizens. Citizens and educators have both the responsibility and the right to make their voices heard so that funds, talents, and resources for which every thinking citizen is responsible are used to educate and rehabilitate rather than to keep millions of fellow human beings in bondage and hopelessness.

The Public School Dropout

Dropouts, or those who leave school as soon as legally possible, number some 700,000 students a year in the United States alone, and the numbers are growing. The problem of high school dropouts has become a major educational issue and concern, as well it should. It is closely related to the preceding discussions about children and it is highly pertinent to the discussion of today's curricular needs which follows this section.

According to Fred M. Hechinger,[7] ". . . most of the widely publicized programs for returning lost sheep to the academic fold appear more concerned with rounding up the strays than with providing the kinds of educational experiences that will encourage them to complete their schooling."

Preventing possible dropouts from living *down* *to* their expectations will require, among other things, significant curriculum revisions and an overhaul of grading concepts, states Dr. Robert D. Strom of Ohio State University. The former associate director of the National Education Association's Project on School Dropouts has written a new booklet, "The Tragic Migration."[8] He points out that slow learners, who include one in five children in the school population, make up the largest group leaving school before graduation. "These students," he comments, "cite as reasons for leaving: lack of interest, inappropriate curriculum, and inability to maintain acceptable grades." If all students are to be kept in school then "it is imperative that *school become relevant*

[7] Fred M. Hechinger, Education Editor, *New York Times,* Sunday, Oct. 25, 1964.
[8] Robert D. Strom, "The Tragic Migration," NEA, 1201 Sixteenth St., N.W., Washington, D.C., 1964.

to all." More specifically, ". . . all required courses must be designed and taught *to meet all ability levels."*

Almost in panic, or else in ignorance or inexperience of the
basic needs of today's students, educators cry for more testing,
more remedial reading and arithmetic, more special classes, more
special-class teachers, more psychiatric help, and more agency
services. They may as well put their shoulders to the wheel and
realize that even if all of these were possible, they might not be
advisable until schools themselves have done a better job, including educating parents to the need for becoming participating part-
ners in the business of education. Further segregation and labeling
are not what is required; what is required are *ideas* that will implement upward mobility among more students and consequently
among more citizens.

The teachers we need today will attempt to tailor imaginative
programs to the special needs of all students, instead of labeling
larger groups of students "special." Teachers like these will alter
old patterns or make new ones, but they will not continue to attempt to force children into a few outmoded molds. They will
question the traditional *Lady of the Lake* and *Evangeline* as the
sole sources of literary inspiration when a *Diary of Anne Frank*
arrives on the scene. And they will create and use new methods
and materials that will interest and motivate the present fifth
of the population that is dropping out of schools because of early
disinterest and failure, as well as the four-fifths who are "marking
time" until graduation.

Today's Curricular Needs

What is meant by school curriculum? To some people, it consists of units of scholarship to be predigested and doled out to
students automatically, whether they need them or not. To others,
it is a textbook program or a course syllabus. To the reading specialist, it is a specific program of sequential skill steps toward
technical reading literacy, and, therefore, the curriculum would

consist largely of such instruction. To the historian, all social-science courses should have an historical basis; and to the economist and the geographer the curriculum should have economic and geographical emphases, respectively.

In the 1965 Charles W. Hunt Lecture of the American Association of Colleges for Teacher Education, Florence B. Stratemeyer spoke on "Perspective on Action in Teacher Education": "Using the power of knowledge to open doors involves a second dimension of scholarship (the first had been *understanding the power of knowledge to open doors*), namely, *having insight into significant relationships* among ideas, phenomena, and events. When the focus is on using knowledge to explore reality and envision new realities of life, it is questionable whether learning to use the methods of the scholar and the basic concepts of *separate* disciplines is adequate. Specialized viewpoints, unless brought into relationship, may well lead to a fragmented view of life. In the world of human affairs, problems and situations do not fall into discreet compartments labeled 'political,' 'economic,' 'historical,' 'aesthetic,' 'technological.' Human affairs call for decisions to be made and require that we draw upon all that we know. Moral issues are part of politics and technology; the world of beauty is integral in many aspects of science."

Largely "the curriculum" has consisted of what has historically dominated schools, and as in so many other areas of living, those who think they benefited from it want to maintain the status quo. It is easy to fall into the assumption that people who cannot master it cannot, therefore, learn. What has really been said is that people who cannot learn what has been set up for them to learn in the manner in which it is taught cannot learn at all. This has been a most unfortunate, unproductive, and narrow way to view school curriculum, and many schools have been, and still are, forced to operate with curriculum dictated long before these times and still perpetuated.

Other professions in modern times have not been afraid to disturb the status quo. In fact, they have deliberately disturbed it, knowing that some risk-taking and disturbances may be the best roads to further progress. Space scientists, for instance, adopt the premise that a failure can become the key to future success if the failing elements are reconstituted and innovations are added. When Mariner Three failed to function on its projected eight-and-one-half-month journey to Mars, it became a $25-million piece of junk orbiting in outer space. But within a few days Mariner Four was on the launching pad! Failure is not only expected occasionally in the worlds of science and industry, it is highly endowed and rewarded, financially and psychologically.

Progress in science and in education needs to be built on intelligent conjectures; failures can provide stepping-stones toward reconstituting elements, making other conjectures, adding innovations, and refocusing in the direction of new attempts and new discoveries. Education, like science, can build on accumulated knowledge, pose new hypotheses, risk colossal failures, cull the successful elements and combinations, and point itself in the direction of new discoveries about man—how he learns; why he thinks and acts as he does; and why he becomes apathetic and inactive. Change is a fact of life, and to be welcomed; nothing else stays the same, and education *cannot stand still*. Risks should not be avoided because of the fear of change or failure.

Past events and current happenings suggest reappraisals that might aid schools in planning strategies. Speaking at the Post-Doctoral Seminar of the College of Education of Ohio State University, A. Harry Passow discussed curriculum for the advantaged as well as for the disadvantaged:[9]

Certainly, the socialization and acculturation functions of the school are of significance to the curriculum planner and his conception of content.

[9] Professor A. Harry Passow of Columbia University from mimeographed copy of his address at the Post-Doctoral Seminar at the College of Education of Ohio State University, October 23, 1964. By permission of Professor Passow.

Obviously, the line of demarcation between content and teaching methodology and resources becomes increasingly blurred for they are interrelated. Teaching strategies may represent methodology but they cannot be divorced from content. . . . For some learnings, the emotional content may have more impact than the cognitive aspects. Or, more significantly, the emotional content may be the vehicle for cognitive learnings.

An anecdote from a Queens College BRIDGE Project science teacher's experience illustrates this point:

Today I decided to begin my unit on the Circulatory System. I began by asking if anyone knew anything about the blood and how it flows through the body. Harold, a transfer, said he knew that blood flowed to all parts of the body. Another boy said that the heart pumps blood, and another said it goes through blue tubes. Before I had a chance to develop the concept of circulation, Harold asked, "Miss M., what kind of guy is real white, whiter than you? He don't have any blood, right?" I knew he meant an albino. I explained that this type of person was an albino but that he had the same kind of blood that we have, and what he is missing is the chemical that makes skin light or dark, —a pigment.

By this time the entire class was completely transfixed upon me and was listening intently to what I was saying. I continued. "Didn't you ever wonder why you are dark and I am light? Why one Negro is much darker than the next? Or why Indians were Redskins, or some Italians have darker skins than Irish people with freckles?" No one said anything. . . . The silence was deadening. I explained that a chemical called pigment determines how light or dark we will be, and that it is passed from one generation to the next along with eye color, hair color and facial contour. I told how this chemical clumps together or scatters, determining whether we are dark or light. Victoria shook the silence with "That ain't true. My mother told us that the reason we is black is that Adam and Eve had two sons, Cain and Abel—Cain was black and Abel white. Because Cain kill Abel, all the black folks like us are bad, and the darker we are, the badder we are." The other kids listened and a few agreed. Several withdraw into their books and Samuel said, "Let's get

on with the lesson." Arthur and William said it wasn't true—"If
that's so, how come so many Negroes do good in the world—
they play music and work at the U.N." Another boy said, "Some
don't do so good; they drink wine all the time. That's how a lot
of us will wind up." Henrietta said, "What about Teen Band
Stand and that ugly old white man, Dick Clark? He always turn
the cameras off the colored kids when they dance. How about
that?" Edward who just moved up North said it wasn't true. He
said, "Whites and Blacks can't be equal and that's the way it is.
My daddy say you gotta live with it that way." William said
rather emotionally, "We don't get the same jobs," and Arnie
said "because wae are dumber than most whites." All this time
I was not in the conversation. Juanita said, "That's why Miss
M. say we should learn a lot so we can get chances our folks
didn't have." The boys wanted the girls to keep quiet.[10]

In this instance, the content which emerges deals more with the
anxieties and emotions of the students than with scientific information. The lesson was experience-centered, in the best sense of that
term. It probably was not in the teacher's plan book but represented
a sensing by her of the genuine concerns of the class. One might observe that this teacher "began where her students were"—a time-
honored but often unpracticed educational dictum which, in the case
of the disadvantaged, is especially crucial. Beginning there has never
implied staying there but, instead, should be the point from which the
teacher educates or leads out. Unfortunately, the anecdote ends without indicating how the teacher helped these pupils conceptualize this
intensive experience.

Later on, Dr. Passow referred to instructional content that
derives from the urban world of today:

There is an instructional content which derives from the urban
world of today with its vast cultural resources as well as its complex
problems. This is sometimes viewed as the subject matter of social
studies, intergroup relations, citizenship education, or some variation
thereof. For example, Ausubel has documented the "significant developmental differences in self-esteem, in aspirations for achievement,

[10] Helen Storen and Robert Edgar, editors, "Learning to Teach in Difficult Schools" (Flushing, N.Y.: Queens College BRIDGE Project, 1963),
p. 39.

in personality adjustment, and in character structure" of segregated Negro children. Together, these two sides of the problem point to a critical aspect of education for the schools which cannot be ignored even though empirical data are lacking which would provide sound guide lines for planning.

The current civil rights struggle, for example, is viewed by some analysts as basically a problem of power redistribution, with some groups seeking to secure power and others to maintain and withhold it. Should the question of political, economic, and social power-re-distribution be part of the legitimate content of social science study of, let us say, secondary school youth? In what ways should the complex, often controversial issues and problems of urban living serve as content for social learnings? These questions do not pose simple reexamination of the handling of controversial issues in the classroom as much as a totally new view of the realities of urban sociopolitical life as they impinge on school curriculum. Perhaps we should be concerned with meaningful citizenship participation, not in terms of boycotts and demonstrations, but rather in helping alienated and disadvantaged children and youth understand the world about them and how they become part of the mainstream of social living. While one can have no illusions about the complexity of selecting and handling content dealing with power relationships in communities, to ignore completely the stresses and strains that are part of America's large cities and metropolitan areas generally is to perpetuate the feeling amongst students that school is divorced from reality. As Kvaraceus has observed rather strongly:

> Since the high school is careful to skirt and detour around real-life problems and controversial issues involving race relations, alcoholism, materialism, religion, politics, collectivism, consumer competency, marriage, and family life, it involves the learner in a type of artificially contrived busy work and shadow boxing that either lulls the adolescent into a stupor or drives him in his resentment out of school to overt aggression. In protecting youth from real-life problems, the school enters into a tragic conspiracy of irresponsible retreat from reality. The perversion of the high school curriculum to neutral and petty purposes emasculates the school program and disintegrates the ego.[11]

[11] William C. Kvaraceus, "Negro Youth and Social Adaptation: The Role of the School as an Agent of Change." Lincoln Filene Center of Tufts University, Medford, Massachusetts. Unpublished Paper.

The school must provide richer opportunities to practice improved modes of behavior as part of the learning experience. What is needed is a reappraisal of the value of real-life experiences in problem-solving and decision-making in the social, political, and economic life of the school and community. The "laboratory-experiences" approach of the Citizenship Education Project may have real meaning here.

A three-year Wilmington (Delaware) project focused directly on the aspect of human relations in an effort to help children and their families comprehend and deal more effectively with changing neighborhoods: transiency, desegregation, flight to the suburbs, and changing economic forces. The focus of curriculum building was on developing human relations sensitivity, skills, insight, and information. Units relating school instruction to life needs and experience were built for specific classes. Such education is viewed as being at the center of the school's program. . . .

Beyond this, there is an intangible content which cannot be ignored, because it is significant in ego-development, in motivation, in self-image. This is what is learned from the classroom climate and the teacher as an individual. How to concoct a climate in which teachers genuinely believe in the potential ability of disadvantaged children, are committed to its nurture, and convey this respect through their relationships with pupils and parents is part and parcel of the curriculum problem. Those writers who observed that the child "learns what he lives" were not off-target. What the teacher expects or does not expect and how the disadvantaged student perceives these expectations can influence significantly the child's aspiration level and involvement in the educational process.

Dale[12] has proposed what he calls a Life Management Curriculum to help students "in the critical choices, the big consequential decisions that they will make during high school and after." The key ingredients in his curriculum would include an overarching concern for the values comprising the good life; attention to effective communication in all its dimensions (reading, observing, listening, speaking, assessing, developing taste and discrimination in literature, music, and the fine arts); concern with improved

[12] Edgar Dale, "Life Management Curriculum," *The Newsletter,* 29: 1–4, Nov. 1963.

mental, emotional, and physical health, including sensitivity to unrelenting pressures from advertising and sales sources; frequent experiences with success in learning as the basis for motivation to learn ("success is the best motivator"); development of a respect for time and its management; help with problems of the consumer in a modern society; and development of effective and responsible work habits, including responsive human relationships and flexibility in a changing technological society.

Dale bases his proposals on the idea that the program must fit the student to living effectively in a complex, changing society. His suggestions call attention to the fact that:

> . . . the critical choices of individuals are not *chiefly* mathematical, linguistic, scientific, or historical. Rather, they are choices of values, of the use of time, energy and money, choices of friends or of a mate, choices in receiving and expressing ideas. They are choices on which one must focus the wisdom in school and out.

The suggestions that have been made in these statements are ideas that express the role and purpose of schools in an urbanized and technological society. The questions now are these. Are we *willing* to look at what we know and begin to modify our techniques, to take differences into account, to modify our instructional materials, and to test new ideas? It seems categorical that the ultimate rewards to the classroom teacher, in terms of the saving of human potential by teaching in the best sense of the word, are inestimable if we are willing to take up the challenge.

Curricular Innovation and New Materials for Intergroup Education

In the preceding descriptions, illustrations, and discussions, it is interesting to note that values, intergroup education, human relations, self-image, and prevailing attitudes are mentioned often. Obviously, curricular recommendations would be for educational programs that insure meaningful growth, provide a sense of attainment and accomplishment, help youngsters understand and face their limitations as well as their strengths, provide for healthy attitudes toward school and society, and generally turn indifference and antagonism, especially of disadvantaged youth, into acceptance and understanding.

There is nothing new about including intergroup education and human relations in curriculum planning, since a study of the turns of the spiral educational emphases would show us that these have been recognized factors in curriculum development since the 1940's. But the kinds of curricula that have been provided in schools have emphasized assimilation and homogeneity of learning experiences and content. However, somewhere along the line it was forgotten entirely, or watered down until it was so acceptable to everyone that we hardly knew it was there. Did the concept of *intergroup* education as curriculum emphasis get lost in the shuffle or fall into disgrace as the spiral of educational emphases took its next turn? Did society think that, once given strong emphasis, it need not be returned to?

A chronic complaint of minority groups is that schools and textbooks ignore minorities' own distinctive pasts and contributions to the majority culture. Minority groups are similarly sensitive to any aspect of literature that presents them in an unfavorable light, as witnessed when some Jewish American groups objected to *The Merchant of Venice,* when Roman Catholic Americans objected to anti-Catholic bias in some history books, and when Negro American groups attacked the use of *Huckleberry Finn* and *Little Black Sambo* in schools.

Some schools systems have attempted to develop their own teaching materials, but it is a rare one that has available the funds and personnel to do this job adequately. Meanwhile, the role of minority groups is belatedly coming into curricular focus, educators are asking for teaching materials that recognize the pluralistic and multi-ethnic nature of our society, and multiple book selections are replacing the single textbook in which scholarly and historical distortions are often predominant.

In an October, 1962, policy statement on textbooks, The Board of Education of New York City reviewed the criticisms of existing textbooks and distorted curriculum practices. Among several evaluative criteria were the following questions:

1. How adequate is the space and treatment given to the roles of various minority groups in our culture?
2. Do the illustrations, both photographs and sketches, reflect the pluralistic nature of our society?
3. Does the treatment reflect the findings of recent historical scholarship?
4. Does the treatment avoid reality by ignoring or glossing over the present-day tensions of intergroup relations and the efforts being made to relieve those tensions?
5. Does the presentation help to promote the goal of a pluralistic society, free from the social ills of discrimination and prejudice in such areas as education, employment, and housing?

Whether multi-ethnic grouping is a factor in one's community or not, one must ask himself what Negro, Puerto Rican, Mexican, Oriental, Indian, and other ethnic groups in America today can find to relate to in books and study materials that present the population of the United States as almost exclusively white, middle-class, Anglo-Saxon or North European in origin, and living in rural or suburban areas. This picture is most certainly at variance with reality, and students who have no opportunity for contact with such groups have no way at all of realizing the true nature of the country and the world in which we live. Students of minority *and* majority groups may decide right from the beginning that school is one thing, and real life quite another—or that real life everywhere is just like the one they know. We can no longer afford to inculcate early disinterest among millions of culturally different children and we cannot afford to present the images we do to American school children or children anywhere else in the world.

Curriculum is *people*—people with ideas and potential; people of all ages and in all states of *being* and *becoming;* people teaching; and people being taught. Curricular innovation that suits today's schools and the schools of the future needs to be a constant quest for the kinds of learning experiences that will help each individual develop his own potentials as he becomes a self-learner and a contributing member of society who will reeducate himself many times in the changing years of his lifetime.

The raw material of teaching and learning, of creating and innovating, is at our command every day in the people who live, learn, teach, work, and function together now and increasingly so in the future.

Summary

We have unprecedented responsibilities to reexamine traditional practices and curricula in schools and in connection with education for citizenship in a democratic society. Questions need to be asked and answered concerning neighborhood concepts; new-migrant dilemmas; the real purposes of schools and education; new needs for educational fulfillment, assumptions about children, the public-school dropout, today's curriculum needs, and curricular innovation that will include new materials for concept formation and intergroup education in today's world.

It becomes necessary to make changes in school programs, for schools—along with the rest of society—must learn to live on the edge of uncertainty and cannot afford to stand still. Bold and imaginative experimentations are needed in education, just as they are in the scientific world. Risk-taking is as important to education as it is to science and industry.

Finally, if all students are to be kept in school, and if we are to educate for wise and satisfying use of time, it is imperative that schools become "relevant for all." John Fischer, President of Teachers College at Columbia University, states emphatically,

The time is now . . . we face an urgent need for basic studies which will involve all we know and can learn through the social and behavioral sciences, in the professional specialties of education, and from every other field of study and experience. To bridge the gap between the culture which the schools traditionally represent and that which character-izes most of the unschooled population of the country calls for cur-ricula, teaching materials, and forms of pedagogical practice which most of our schools have scarcely dreamed of, much less developed. But the need for new knowledge in no way justifies delay in using what we now know, or what we are able now to do, imperfect and incomplete though these may be. . . .

But we must constantly emphasize the essential importance of bring-ing children of all races into schools together. Action to accomplish this must be taken deliberately, systematically, and rapidly wherever it can be taken without clear damage to the educational opportuni-ties of children involved.[13]

[13] John H. Fischer, "The Inclusive School," *Teachers College Record,* October 1964, p. 4.

CHAPTER **2**

CIVIL RIGHTS AND
INTERGROUP RELATIONS

THE Civil Rights Act of 1964 was the most far-reaching and definitive action in the protection of civil rights taken by the United States Congress for nearly one hundred years. It set up procedures to *enforce* the constitutional right to vote, to confer jurisdiction upon the district courts of the United States to provide relief against discrimination in public accommodations, to authorize the Attorney General to institute suits to protect constitutional rights in *public facilities* and *public education,* to extend the United States Commission on Civil Rights, to prevent discrimination in federally assisted programs, and to establish a Commission on Equal Employment Opportunity and Community Relations Services.

"Civil rights," as the term is generally used, means the right to be treated equally, regardless of one's race, color, ancestry, or religion. This "right" protects against discrimination not only in the exercise of constitutional rights such as voting, but also in jobs, housing, public accommodations, education, and other areas of life.

The Supreme Court decision of 1954 stated that racially segregated schools deny "the equal protection of the laws" guaranteed by the Fourteenth Amendment. A year later the court ordered the school districts involved in the cases before it to desegregate their facilities "with all deliberate speed." Yet in Greenville, Mississippi, it took until January of 1965 for the Greenville School Board to vote unanimously to prepare a desegregation plan to comply with the Civil Rights Act and the clause affecting federal aid to education. Then the action followed a warning by the school board president that "if we let this go by default, it will be done for us." Greenville, in the heart of Mississippi's rich cotton-growing delta, faced the loss of nearly three hundred thousand dollars in federal education funds if it failed to comply with the civil rights law.

The mayor of this city endorsed the board's action, but reluctantly, saying that there was no alternative. "Repugnant as the law is to all of us, it's a federal law and it's either a case of comply or close the schools," he said. In the state of Mississippi, Greenville became the fifth school district to prepare an integration plan. The other four had acted under federal court orders. School board attorney Edgar Bogen told the board that it had only two choices—to comply with the act or defy the law and wait for legal action to be instigated; and the president of the board emphasized the fact that the *real* choice was whether the community obeyed the law *with* federal aid or *without* federal aid.

In an address delivered to the American people by President John F. Kennedy on June 11, 1963, he said:

This afternoon, following a series of threats and defiant statements, the presence of Alabama National Guardsmen was required on the University of Alabama to carry out the final and unequivocal order of the United States District Court of the Northern District of Alabama. That order called for the admission of two clearly qualified young Alabama residents who happened to have been born Negro. That they were admitted peacefully on the campus is due in good measure to the conduct of the students of the University of Alabama who met their responsibilities in a constructive way. I hope that every

American, regardless of where he lives, will stop and examine his conscience about this and other related incidents.

Speaking of *the rights of all men,* he continued:

This nation was founded by men of many nations and backgrounds. It was founded on the principle that all men are created equal, and that the rights of every man are diminished when the rights of one man are threatened. Today we are committed to a worldwide struggle to promote and protect the rights of all who wish to be free. And when Americans are sent to Vietnam or West Berlin we do not ask for whites only.

It ought to be possible, therefore, for American students of any color to attend any public institution they select without having to be backed up by troops. It ought to be possible for American consumers of any color to receive equal service in places of public accommodation, such as hotels and restaurants, and theaters and retail stores without being forced to resort to demonstrations in the street.

And it ought to be possible for American citizens of any color to register and vote in a free election without interference or fear of reprisal.

It ought to be possible, in short, for every American to enjoy the privileges of being American without regard to his race or his color.

The plight of Afro-Americans was expressed in this address as follows:

The Negro baby born in America today, regardless of the section or the state in which he is born, has about one-half as much chance of completing high school as a white baby, born in the same place, on the same day; one-third as much chance of completing college; one-third as much chance of becoming a professional man; twice as much chance of becoming unemployed; about one-seventh as much chance of earning $10,000 a year; a life expectancy which is seven years shorter and the prospects of earning only half as much.

This is not a sectional issue. Difficulties over segregation and discrimination exist in every city, in every state of the Union, producing in many cities a rising tide of discontent that threatens the public safety. . . . One hundred years of delay have passed since President Lincoln freed the slaves, yet their heirs, their grandsons, are not fully free. They are not yet freed from the bonds of injustice; they are not yet freed from social and economic oppression.

He raised the question America must face as he continued,

We preach freedom around the world, and we mean it. And we cherish our freedom here at home. But are we to say to the world— and much more importantly to each other—that this is the land of the free, except for the Negroes; that we have no second-class citizens, except Negroes; that we have no class or caste system, no ghettos, no master race, except with respect to Negroes?

Now the time has come for this nation to fulfill its promise. The events in Birmingham and elsewhere have so increased the cries for equality that no city or state or legislative body can prudently choose to ignore them. The fires of frustration and discord are burning in every city, North and South. Where legal remedies are not at hand, redress is sought in the streets in demonstrations, parades and protests, which create tensions and threaten violence—and threaten lives.

Referring to the fact that the following week he would ask the Congress of the United States to make a commitment that it had not fully made in this century, he said the action needed was a rededication

. . . to the proposition that race has no place in American life or law. The Federal judiciary has upheld that proposition in a series of forthright cases. The Executive Branch has adopted that proposition in the conduct of its affairs, including the employment of Federal personnel, and the use of Federal facilities, and the sale of Federally financed housing.

Saying that legislation cannot solve problems of discrimination alone, President Kennedy continued, *"It must be solved in the home of every American in every community across our country."*

The remainder of this valuable contribution to our heritage follows:

In this respect, I want to pay tribute to those citizens, North and South, who have been working in their communities to make life better for all. They are acting not out of a sense of legal duty but out of a sense of human decency. Like our soldiers and sailors in all parts of the world, they are meeting freedom's challenge on the firing line and I salute them for their honor—their courage.

My fellow Americans, this is a problem which faces us all, in every city of the North as well as the South. Today there are Negroes unemployed—two or three times as many compared to whites; inadequate education; moving into the large cities, unable to find work; young people particularly out of work, without hope, denied equal rights, denied the opportunity to eat at a restaurant or lunch counter, or go to a movie theater; denied the right to a decent education; denied almost, today, the right to attend a state university even though qualified.

It seems to me that these are matters which concern us all—not merely Presidents, or congressmen, or governors, but every citizen of the United States.

This is one country. It has become one country because all of us and all the people who came here had an equal chance to develop their talents. We cannot say to ten percent of the population that "you can't have that right. Your children can't have the chance to develop whatever talents they have, that the only way that they are going to get their rights is to go in the street and demonstrate." I think we owe them and we owe ourselves a better country than that.

Therefore, I am asking for your help in making it easier for us to move ahead and provide the kind of equality of treatment which we would want ourselves—to give a chance for every child to be educated to the limit of his talent.

As I have said before, not every child has an equal talent or an equal ability or equal motivation. But they should have the equal *right* to develop their talent and their ability and their motivation to make something of themselves. We have a right to expect that the Negro community will be responsible, will uphold the law. But *they* have a right to expect that the law will be fair, that the Constitution will be color-blind, as Justice Harlan said at the turn of the century. This is what we are talking about. This is a matter which concerns this country and what it stands for, and in meeting it I ask the support of all of our citizens.

History has given us a President, Lyndon B. Johnson, who is, with the aid of the American people through their elected representatives, translating these words into action. When Lyndon B. Johnson said, after President Kennedy's tragic assassination, "Let's get this plane back to Washington," he meant much more than the physical transposition. The actions and deeds of Congress since that fateful day have borne out the promise that *every* American child may begin to have *equal* opportunity.

The Law and Intergroup Relations

On many occasions throughout American history it has been found necessary to translate lofty theories into more concrete terms. Building a nation, or even one school, upon solid democratic foundations was never accomplished easily.

From the very beginning of our national existence, Americans have stated in unmistakable terms that *all men are created equal* —that each is endowed with the same inalienable rights. Long before these commitments, our spiritual forefathers elevated the doctrine that each man is his brother's keeper—that all men share a common obligation to love their neighbors as themselves. Americans cannot be honest with themselves if they treat these doctrines as inapplicable to all situations. In our time, the dictum is inescapable. In our time, no American can afford to say that either our spiritual or our legal heritage is "repugnant."

At the federal level of government, there have been constitutional amendments, Supreme Court rulings, and Executive orders that bring us to a confrontation of our responsibilities. To fill the gaps between our principles and our practices will require commitment and action by all agencies, but *the single best means we possess is our schools.*

Although the Fourteenth Amendment of the United States Constitution, adopted shortly after the Civil War, provides that no state "may deny any person within its jurisdiction the equal protection of the laws," the Supreme Court decision of 1954[1] stated that racially segregated schools *deny* "the equal protection of the laws" guaranteed by the Fourteenth Amendment.

A year later the Court ordered the school districts involved in the cases before it to desegregate their facilities "with all deliberate speed."[2] The Civil Rights Acts of 1957[3] and 1960[4] enabled

[1] Brown v. Board of Education, 347 U.S. 459 (1954).
[2] Brown v. Board of Education, 349 U.S. 298–301 (1955).
[3] Civil Rights Act of 1957, 71 Stat. 637, 42 U.S.C. sec 1971 (1958).
[4] Civil Rights Act of 1960, 74 Stat. 86, 42 U.S.C., sec 1971 (1960).

the United States Department of Justice to take action to protect the voting rights of Negroes, while Executive orders issued by Presidents Roosevelt, Truman, Eisenhower, and Kennedy required companies doing business with the Federal Government to practice nondiscrimination in hiring workers.

The passing of civil rights legislation in 1964 under the leadership of President Lyndon B. Johnson has paved the way for actions and commitments that should have taken place long ago in this country's history. The Economic Opportunity Act of 1964[5] declares in Section 2:

The United States can achieve its full economic and social potential as a nation only if every individual has the opportunity to contribute to the full extent of his capabilities, and to participate in the workings of our society. It is, therefore, the policy of the United States to eliminate the paradox of poverty in the midst of plenty in this Nation by opening to everyone the opportunity for education and training, the opportunity to work, and the opportunity to live in decency and dignity. It is the purpose of this Act to strengthen, supplement, and coordinate efforts in furtherance of that policy.

The mere enactment of laws has not yet, and will not for a long time, fully protect citizens against discrimination because of race, color, religion, ancestry, or national origin in the important areas of securing an education, getting a job, locating a house or apartment, or obtaining equal service in places of public accommodation.

Even the party platforms of the 1964 election were built upon gnarly issues that will plague our courts for many years at local and national levels. The Democratic Party's 1964 Platform included this declaration:[6]

The variety of our people is the source of our strength and ought not to be the cause of disunity and discord. The rights of all our citi-

---

[5] Public Law 88–452, 88th Congress, S. 2642, August 20, 1964 (1964).
[6] From official text of the Democratic Party Platform, formally adopted at the party's Convention in Atlantic City, N.J., August 25, 1964.

zens must be protected and all the laws of our land obeyed if America is to be safe for democracy.

The Civil Rights Act of 1964 deserves and requires full observance by every American and fair, effective enforcement if there is any default.

Resting upon a national consensus expressed by the overwhelming support of both parties, this new law impairs the rights of no American; it affirms the rights of all Americans. Its purpose is not to divide, but to end division; not to curtail the opportunities of any, but to increase opportunities for all; not to punish, but to promote further commitment to freedom, the pursuit of justice, and a deeper respect for human dignity.

We reaffirm our belief that lawless disregard for the rights of others is wrong—whether used to deny equal rights or to obtain equal rights.

We cannot and will not tolerate lawlessness. We can and will seek to eliminate its economic and social causes.

True democracy of opportunity will not be served by establishing quotas based on the same false distinctions we seek to erase, nor can the effects of prejudice be neutralized by the expedient of preferential practices.

With special references to our Indian citizens, older citizens, younger citizens, equality of opportunity for women as well as men, and revision of immigration laws, the following statement was made:

Ending discrimination based on race, age, sex, or national origin demands not only equal opportunity but the opportunity to be equal. We are concerned not only with people's right to be free, but also their ability to use their freedom.

The States and Federal Law

States Rights, long the option of those areas not covered specifically by Federal laws, have perpetuated discrimination and injustices in many parts of our country. But at the state level, too, legislation has progressively underlined constitutional guarantees of equal rights.

In Connecticut, for instance, when the Fourteenth Amendment to the United States Constitution was adopted shortly after the Civil War, providing that no state may "deny to any person within its jurisdiction the equal protection of the laws," the state was the first to ratify the amendment. The Connecticut State Constitution of 1818 declares that all men are equal in rights and guarantees freedom of religion, speech, press, and assembly.

In 1868 the Connecticut legislature opened the public schools of the state to all children regardless of their race or color. The Twenty-third Amendment to the Connecticut Constitution of 1876 eliminated the requirement that voters be white. By 1884, depriving anyone of his constitutional or legal rights because of alienage, color, or race became punishable by fine or imprisonment or both. In 1917 the General Assembly provided for fine or imprisonment or both of any person who "by his advertisement ridicules or holds up to contempt any person or class of persons on account of creed, religion, color, denomination, nationality or race." In 1949, discrimination, including segregation, on account of race, creed, or color was prohibited in the armed forces of the state.[7]

Civil rights related to employment have been progressively defined in Connecticut law, and a means of enforcing fair employment practices has been provided. In 1937, the State Merit System Act, governing employment by the State, forbade discrimination against anyone in appointments, demotions, or dismissals to or from state jobs because of political or religious opinions or affiliations, or because of color.

In 1943, the governor was authorized to appoint ten commissioners to a new government agency, the Connecticut Interracial Commission, the first such state body in the country. It was made responsible for examining and compiling facts on discrimination

[7] Information used in this section through the courtesy of Elizabeth Krom, Supervisor Intergroup Division, Commission on Civil Rights, State of Connecticut.

in employment, violations of civil liberties, and other related matters. Its findings led it to a recommendation of passage of a Fair Employment Practices Act. Connecticut's FEP Act, passed in 1947, was the fourth in the nation. It bars any discrimination in employment based on a worker's race, color, religious creed, national origin, or ancestry, or, since 1959, on age of forty to sixty-five years inclusive.

The Connecticut Commission on Civil Rights (the name given to the Connecticut Interracial Commission in 1951) enforces the FEP Act. A worker who feels that he has been discriminated against can complain to the Commission which in turn must make an investigation and attempt to settle the matter privately. If the Commission finds that discrimination has existed and has not been eliminated during these negotiations, it must proceed with a full public hearing, at which the State Attorney General speaks for the complainant, makes a finding, and if necessary, gets a court order to enforce its decisions. So, too, an appeal to the courts may be taken by a worker whose complaint the Commission has dismissed or by an employer, union, employment agency, or other persons charged with discrimination. The Commission itself has the power to initiate complaints.

This Commission on Civil Rights in Connecticut consists of ten commissioners, appointed by the governor for five-year terms, who serve without pay and supervise the Commission's work. The staff for this work is employed under the State Merit System. The three divisions of the Commission that carry out the functions assigned to it are: Enforcement and Conciliation; Research; and Intergroup Relations.

In 1949, Connecticut became the first state to hold a public hearing under a Fair Employment Practices Law, and when the finding for the complainant was appealed in Superior Court, it was the first court test of these laws. Again, in 1950, in a case that lasted nearly four years, the Commission proceeded to a hearing over the refusal of a labor union to admit two Negroes as apprentices. The union was fined a large sum outright and ordered to pay $500 weekly until the two Negroes were admitted to union apprenticeship. The invoking of a contempt proceeding by the Commission was also a "first."

The City of New Haven adopted fair employment practice ordinances with enforcement powers exceeding those of the Commission on Civil Rights in the early 1960's; other municipalities made official statements confirming the fact that the State's anti-discrimination laws were the official policy of their communities.

Action taken by states such as Pennsylvania caused the 1955 Legislature to create a Fair Employment Practice Commission known as FEPC, and in 1961 this law was amended by the Human Relations Act to cover, in addition to employment, the areas of housing and public accommodations. The Human Relations Act makes it unlawful to discriminate because of race, color, religion, ancestry, or national origin in any part of the employment process, in providing equal service in places of public accommodation, and in the selling, renting, or financing of housing; it is specific also about unlawful practices in each of the areas covered by the law.[8]

Pennsylvania and Connecticut, like the majority of northern and midwestern states, had early statutes (passed in Connecticut in 1905) that guaranteed equal services in public places, and forbade discrimination because of race, color, religion, ancestry, or national origin in the admission of students to colleges and universities, and to secretarial, business, vocational, or trade schools. In Pennsylvania, the Civil Rights Law regarding equal educational opportunities is administered by the Human Relations Commission.[9]

Although Pennsylvania has a set of civil rights laws not sur-

[8] Pennsylvania State Legislature, Act. No. 19, Feb. 28, 1961, P.L. 47.
[9] Information used in the section relating to Pennsylvania through the courtesy of Frank D. Davis, Director of Publicity and Information, Pennsylvania Human Relations Commission, Commonwealth of Pennsylvania.

passed in scope by any other state and, like Connecticut, showed early and consistent legislation to improve discriminatory practices, its 1939 Civil Rights Law codifying all preexisting Commonwealth laws that dealt with discrimination in public accommodations was severely limited in effectiveness where there were hard-core areas of discrimination. There were two reasons for this:

1. The Civil Rights Law, a part of the State's criminal code, required a person injured by discrimination to go to the office of an alderman, justice of the peace, or magistrate to swear out a warrant for arrest, or to induce the county district attorney to issue information, with attendant fees and legal involvement.

2. Many times the injured person found it impossible to locate an alderman, justice of the peace, or magistrate willing to accept the handling of his complaint, and, if the complaint were not settled at that level, grand juries, reflecting local majority group sentiment, generally refused to indict the offending proprietor.

Between 1939 and 1955, Pennsylvania's civil rights guarantees were strengthened by additional laws. Here are a few examples:

1. No question in any civil service examination may relate to the race or religion of a candidate.[10]

2. No person in the classified civil service may be removed, except for just cause, which cannot be his race or religion.[11]

3. No discrimination may be exercised, threatened or promised by any person against or in favor of any applicant to or employee of the police force, because of religious opinions or affiliation or race.[12]

4. It is unlawful for any school director, superintendent or

[10] Act of August 5, 1941, P.L. Commonwealth of Pennsylvania, 752.
[11] Act of August 5, 1941, P.L. Commonwealth of Pennsylvania, 752.
[12] Act of May 1, 1927, P.L. Commonwealth of Pennsylvania, 519.

teacher in any public school to make any distinction whatever, on account of, or by reason of the race or color of any
pupil or scholar attending a public school or seeking admission to it.[13]

5. Every contract with the Commonwealth or any of its sub-
divisions, including school districts, for public work must
contain a provision by which the contractor agrees that
neither he nor any subcontractor will discriminate in the
hiring of employees because of race, creed or color.[14]

Even though citizens in most northern and midwestern states
today enjoy some protection against discrimination because of
race, color, religion, ancestry, or national origin in the important
areas of securing an education, getting a job, locating a house or
apartment, and obtaining equal service in public places, it is well
for the student of democracy to consider why and how these laws
came about. Each was born of necessity to spell out the original
promises of the new American Republic. Each became necessary
in addition to the United States Constitution, so that the member
states of the Union would not interpret unjustly the rights that
they considered to be theirs. And in the states where such laws
never existed—where indeed many human beings were considered
to be the chattel of other human beings—these freedoms were no
more than words on paper for millions of Americans. Notably in
some of our western states and especially in southern states, there
were no such protections or intentions.

Contrasting State Interpretations

Although we are apt to think of discrimination as a factor prevalent only in the southern United States, in California, during the
1964 political campaigns, an existing state law on fair housing

[13] Act of March 10, 1949, P.L. Commonwealth of Pennsylvania, 30.
[14] Act of July 18, 1935, P.L. Commonwealth of Pennsylvania, 1173.

was a major campaign issue. The 1963 law forbade discrimination on the basis of race, color, religion, national origin, or ancestry in the sale and rental of housing, but Proposition 14 on the 1964 ballot was for *repeal of this law*. California's voters said "Yes," and the 1963 law was repealed. So we cannot assume that laws that have been hard won and are now a reality cannot be repealed when bigoted groups become dominant in state politics.

Proposition 14 created a new property right in the California State Constitution: the "right" of an owner or his agent to sell or rent to anyone "as he in his absolute discretion chooses." Backers of Proposition 14, which was sponsored by the California Real Estate Association, argue that a citizen should have "freedom to rent or sell to whom he chooses." Opponents, of which there were obviously not enough to defeat the proposition, contended that passage would "legislate hate" and do away with many gains in the field of better race relations.

Such an issue can be appealed to the courts either on the ground that it illegally revises the state constitution, or on the ground that it conflicts with the Fourteenth Amendment of the United States Constitution. In any case, it is a classic example of the fact that for generations, children in our country have been taught that "all men are created equal," even while they are being taught just as thoroughly that "it is not desirable to live next door to people of certain races and religions." School people continue to agree that "children should be taught to understand and appreciate the ideals of American democracy, without ever examining the built-in contradictions in our society or discovering how to help children and adults resolve them creatively."[15]

Segregated housing creates segregated neighborhood schools, and the problem of unscrambling segregated neighborhoods and of creating educational parks where children from many neighborhoods can attend school together is taking far too long.

[15] Charlotte Epstein, *The Bulletin* of the National Association of Secondary School Principals, October, 1960.

The New York State Department of Education has declared that "the common school has long been viewed as a basic social instrument in attaining our traditional American goals of equal opportunity and personal fulfillment," and it has asserted as a guiding principle for all school systems in the state:

The presence of a single school of children from varied racial, cultural, socioeconomic, and religious backgrounds is an important element in the preparation of young people for active participation in the social and political affairs of our democracy.[16]

It would be impossible here to cite the recurring incidents that represent the defiance of civil rights laws, and that have always represented a threat to human decency and equal opportunity. Some classic examples can be found both north and south of the Mason-Dixon line.

The record of American schools in providing opportunities for educationally disadvantaged children is far from impressive. The past ten or fifteen years have brought many shocking examples of the results of prejudice passed from generation to generation. The Little Rocks and Selmas have been many, showing that old hatreds are deep and abiding.

Among the most well-known and prolonged examples of refusal to comply with Federal Court orders was the Prince Edward County closure of all public schools in 1959. Prince Edward County is south of the Mason-Dixon line in the southside country of Virginia, and will be remembered as one of the country's most stubborn and provincial counties.

Virginia's nearly one million Negroes, many of whom are a captured people, serve as a cheap labor force to the white land and business owners. Their pay rarely exceeds the minimum wage, and their employment is spasmodic. The annual family income in Prince Edward County is less than two thousand dollars a year;

[16] New York State Education Commission's Advisory Committee on Human Relations and Community Tensions, "Guiding Principles for Securing Racial Balance in Public Schools," June 17, 1963.

people are shabbily dressed and underfed; their health problems are ignored and their life expectancy is sixty-four years against their white brother's seventy. If ever there were a corner of the United States where good education was so desperately needed, it was in Prince Edward County, Virginia.

But in 1959, the public schools there closed their doors entirely rather than desegregate. Previous to 1959, Negro children attended schools that were separate and far from equal. They had no library facilities, buildings were dilapidated and had no adequate sanitary facilities. They even lacked materials necessary for instruction. They were, of course, staffed by Negro teachers only, who were assigned to them not because they were poorly educated, but because they were Negro. Negro teachers did not teach in white schools just as Negro children did not go to the modern, well-equipped white schools. Negro children remained in these schools until they could find employment, and they were unmotivated to attend upper academic or trade schools, most of which were not available to them, anyway.

After the schools were closed, they remained inactive and locked for four long years. White parents sent their children to private and parochial schools; Negroes who could moved north, but the vast majority existed in their misery without even the advantage of schooling. These four years of their lives can never be made up; not only were the skills they had learned lost and forgotten, but no new ones were gained. Antipathies should, and do, run deep in the hearts of those whom society forgets.

In 1963, the schools were reopened under the auspices of the Prince Edward Project. However, Neil V. Sullivan, the Superintendent of Schools who was engaged to head the project of getting the schools reopened and functioning again, suggests that the children not only captured some lost skills and began acquiring new ones faster than most groups, but "an important fringe benefit accrued to both the children and then the professional staff in losing the color concept. It was first lost by the children and then by the professional staff. If no reward other than this resulted from the Prince Edward Project (1963–64), all participants would have felt richly rewarded for their involvement."[17]

Among Mr. Sullivan's recommendations, as among those of leading educators from both the North and South, are emphases on courses in intergroup education for students, teachers, and laymen; and widespread knowledge of the irreparable damage to generations of youth denied educational and economic opportunities.

When schools fail to relate the ideals of freedom, equality, and democracy to children's worlds, what others call the "American way of life" must remain for them a fiction and a fraud. A community or a state that will not support decent schools for its children—all of its children—can hardly expect those children to become responsible, contributing men and women.

De Facto Segregation—Some Recommendations

There are many organizations that have had long-standing commitments to equality of opportunity in public life and have worked ceaselessly to promote associations among groups of adults and children that will emphasize and honor group differences. Those of us working in public schools have long recognized that the strategic and unique position of the public school in American life makes it an ideal instrumentality for representation of rich cross-sections of American pluralisms.

Many of us have urged public school districting that would create diversified rather than homogeneous student bodies through experimentation with *school district boundary revision, inter-neighborhood site selection, pupil and teacher transfer, pairing of schools* (for instance, two middle schools so that students in Grades 4–5 go to one school, and Grades 6–7 or 7–8 to another),

[17] Neil V. Sullivan, *Saturday Review,* Oct. 17, 1964, pp. 60–61.

and many other plans and procedures that could help public schools realize the value and import of integration and diversity as positive factors in educating for democracy.

The National Community Relations Advisory Council[18] has recently published a paper that states the position of this agency in clear, concise, and provocative terms. Saying that the statement is being issued at this time "because the need for action now to alleviate the entrenched evils of *de facto* segregation in public schools is urgent," and because "issues that have become obscured and confused require clarification," it further emphasizes that racial segregation "is antithetical to democracy," and that "its deliberate cultivation or perpetuation is a blatant repudiation of the root ideas of democracy."

Publications of many national groups emphasize the fact that racial integration in public schools is an essential component of good education in our society, and that integration itself is neither a substitute for nor an alternative to quality education.

The United States Supreme Court rulings cited earlier in this chapter have emphasized the Brown Case[19] ruling ("separation of some children from others of similar age and qualification because of their race generates a feeling of inferiority as to their status that may affect their hearts and minds in a way unlikely ever to be undone"), and it becomes increasingly obvious that it is impossible to have separate but equal education. Whether segregation is imposed by law, or custom, or circumstance, motivation and ability are impaired in the stigmatization of isolation.

In the education and selection of teachers and in the policies that govern schools, there needs to be increased emphasis on the ideal that quality education and racial and ethnic integration are mutually complementary and interdependent. In the NCRAC

[18] National Community Relations Advisory Council,"*De Facto* Segregation in Public Schools—A Position Paper," NCRAC, October 18, 1964.
[19] Brown v. Board of Education 347 U.S. 495 (1954) and Brown v. Board of Education 349 U.S. 298–301 (1955).

paper the following statement is made: "The white child attending a segregated school, which by its racial exclusiveness implicitly reaffirms and reinforces the myth of inherent white superiority, is scarcely being prepared ideally for effective living in a society made up of different racial groups." Further, the white child is certainly not being prepared for living in a world in which he is a minority and not a majority group member.

Racial segregation is just as prevalent in the North as it is in the South, due to patterns of occupational and housing segregation. Among the key issues mentioned earlier in this book are *sharpened economic stratifications, flight of middle-class families to the suburbs,* and *substantial movements of white pupils to nonpublic schools.*

It has become abundantly clear also that with a few notable exceptions, Negro schools in the North and the South are slum schools. They are not only racially segregated, but buildings are old, physically dilapidated, poorly equipped, understaffed, and overcrowded. In these schools we find the largest turnover, the greatest proportions of uncertified and substitute teachers, and curricula, teaching methods, and instructional materials that are irrevelant to the lives and experiences of these children.

Among the collective remedial recommendations of many groups are the following:

1. The creation of school parks or school campuses that will include many grade levels and draw students from extensive geographic areas. This recommendation has the advantage of pooling facilities, talents, and resources (financial, human, and material) so that they can be used in one geographic area. This also involves site selection for new school construction that will draw from different economic, ethnic, and racial pupil populations.

2. The pairing or other types of grouping (as explained earlier) where schools already exist in segregated neighborhoods.

3. Changing patterns of movement from lower level to higher level schools; for instance, the Princeton Plan houses primary (K–2) students in one complex, Grades 3–4 in another, 5–6 in another. Some school districts are returning to the former 4–4–4 plan. This involves locating Grades K–4, 5–8, 9–12 complexes in strategic multi-ethnic and varied socioeconomic areas.

4. Revising school district boundaries to provide for newly created diverse groupings.

5. Enriching the curricular offerings and special educational services is especially important. This enrichment includes provision for smaller classes, curricular materials and textbooks adapted to the needs of today's students, better counseling services and testing procedures, revision of materials to determine students' real potentials beyond conventional scholastic aptitudes, more adult education programs, involvement of parents and students in motivational programs, summer and after-school enrichment programs, preschool education for children from culturally disadvantaged homes, and use of schools as community schools available to groups of all ages, for the entire calendar year.

Community leaders and educators should consider and act upon these kinds of recommendations *before* strife, community conflict, and pressure have made themselves felt. Taken in the midst of pressure and necessity for change, politics frequently become involved, and counterpressures compound the problems that we seek to resolve.

Too many professional educators and Boards of Education are not exercising the leadership necessary to meet the greatest educational challenge of these times. They are afraid to commit themselves to school desegregation as a factor in quality education. The fear sometimes stems from job insecurity, and in this respect educators and Boards of Education need the widest possible support and intelligent participation of community agencies and lay groups.

It is the thesis of this book that *intergroup* education must be considered a necessary component of quality education when physical desegregation has taken place, and particularly where it has *not* taken place.

Public schools have an obligation to lead children toward ways of thinking and feeling about people that will help create a natural regard for each individual. Public schools must develop appropriate programs of instruction and attitude formation that will lead all citizens, young and old, to accept differences and to judge each person on his individual contributions and worth *as a person*. The climate of each school is set by teachers and supervisors; and the climate that fosters intergroup education is expressed in the curriculum, translated into practice in the classroom, and manifested in relationships among pupils and teachers and administrators. The climate, therefore, is a reflection of the commitment of a community and the schools that represent it.

Essential to this climate is continuity in teacher preservice and inservice education. Teachers' colleges and inservice training programs do not presently prepare teachers to understand class and caste in our society; nor do they adequately prepare teachers for the role they must play in social change and conflict. Few have had specific training in anthropology, sociology, economics, or psychology to prepare them adequately for the real-life situations they will be facing and in which they can make substantial contributions. Changed teaching techniques, methods of understanding aspirations and fears of culturally different children, and the ability to innovate are qualities that are needed and should be fostered. Subject matter mastery is useless without the accompanying attitudes and behaviors that are critical components in any educational program.

Teachers, like social workers and other public employees, should be assigned to positions in accordance with the needs and requirements of a school system; periodically, they should prob-ably be rotated. This meets with great teacher resistance, and teacher preferences should be considered; but teachers should not be allowed to have a vested right in one particular school, and should be willing to share their talents and competencies. This applies to principals and other school administrators and super-visors as well.

Intergroup education for today's schools, then, involves many elements and many people. Teachers' colleges, community agen-cies, school policy-makers, public school administrators, teach-ers, children, parents—all are responsible for initiating coopera-tive programs. This will require coordinated efforts, soul searching, intelligent analysis, and dynamic and creative actions.

The policies and behaviors essential to a democratic society in-volve much more than casual contact among people of differing creeds and races. Deliberate, planned, and sequentially defensible procedures are recommended and required. A decade after the 1954 Supreme Court decisions, and nearly three and one-half cen-turies after the first slaves were brought to United States shores, our society needs to right the inequities and educational short-comings long overdue in a democracy.

Until these inequities are righted, the laws of our land remain empty words and unfulfilled promises. We live in a world where no race can afford to set itself apart or be set apart. In the search for useful criteria to carry us forward to education that is genuine and truly universal, it would be hard to find a better standard than the one John Dewey gave America at the turn of this century:

What the best and wisest parent wants for his own child, that must the community want for all of its children. Any other ideal for our schools is narrow and unlovely; acted upon, it destroys our democ-racy.

CHAPTER **3**

PREJUDICE, STEREOTYPING, AND ETHNOCENTRISM

WHAT is prejudice? stereotyping? ethnocentrism? Are these attitudes and values found among both majority and minority groups? How often do adults discuss the implications of group membership with children? Has traditional education proved to be an effective antidote? Can people unlearn these attitudes? Can schools counteract regional and provincial prejudices? What are the effects of intergroup associations?

These are questions that need to be asked as we investigate research concerning the nature of prejudice, its effect upon people, and the possible role that education can play in its prevention and treatment. Once the *causes* of prejudice and discrimination are clearly understood, perhaps it will be possible to proceed to effective countermeasures to intragroup and intergroup hostilities that cripple real perception and affect the daily lives of otherwise capable people. Especially in schools, the teacher is the person who most affects the life of each student. Consequently it is *essential* that every citizen-teacher understand the nature of prejudice in order to participate in planning effective procedures to deal with it in an educational way.

Probably the most complete *definition* of prejudice has been given by Gordon W. Allport, Professor of Psychology at Harvard University:[1]

Ethnic prejudice is an antipathy based upon a faulty and inflexible generalization. It may be expressed. It may be directed toward a group as a whole, or toward an individual because he is a member of that group.

Prof. Allport also cites the basic fallacy of prejudice:

There is probably not a single instance where every member of a group has all the characteristics ascribed to this group, nor is there a single characteristic that is typical of every member of one group and of no other group.

A common corollary of prejudice is *ethnocentrism*. This is the attitude by which we look with uncritical favor upon the ways of our own group, and judge others by the values of our own. The familiar ways of one's own group are not only thought to be superior to the less familiar ways of other groups, but are also thought to be right and natural. In the extreme, it is believing that the ways of one's group are the best and that the ways of other groups are unnatural and inferior.

Consequently, ethnocentrism causes stereotyping not only of one's own group, but also of other groups. It cripples the ability to judge each person on his own individual worth and achievements. It also blocks intragroup and intergroup understanding and co-operation.

How Early Does Prejudice Begin?

It may be correctly assumed that no child is born prejudiced and that prejudices are acquired somewhere in the process of ac-culturation and association. However, the extent of *racial aware-*

[1] Gordon W. Allport, *The Nature of Prejudice* (Addison-Wesley Pub. Co., 1954).

ness and *intergroup rejection* in very young children is often underestimated.

Jean was a first-year teacher in a medium-sized New England city when she faced her class of all-Negro second-graders on the beginning day. She said that she learned more during the first six months on the job than she had in the entire preceding four years of college; and she expressed the wish that her preservice training could have prepared her more adequately to understand and help her students.

For one thing, Jean learned that her small charges did not hold a very high opinion of *themselves*. When they were angry or upset, they called each other "black," "son of a nigger," and worse. When they were angry at the teacher, they called her "black," too, but never to her face. Youthful tattlers reported name-calling to the playground teacher by announcing, "Jimmy called you an *awful* name outside—he called you *black!*"

The day Jean wore new brown lace stockings—an extravagance purchased with one of her first pay checks—the children were obviously upset about them. When she asked why they didn't like them, one child spoke for the group when she said, "Because they make you look black, like us!"

For another thing, Jean realized that these children already harbored antipathies toward white children and toward white adults, with the exception of "teacher." These feelings and attitudes came to light when Jean brought news clippings about the city's pupil population shifts to effect better racial balance and more equal educational facilities. She read parts of the clippings and then used this information to start a discussion by asking: "Would you like to have some white children come to this school?" With one voice, the class responded in negative terms. The same response was given when she asked whether they would like to attend a neighboring (white) school. Reasons for these negative responses included "Because we don't like them!" "They hate us!" "They think they're smarter than we are!" "They're Jews and Wops over there!"

Discussion disclosed that none of the reactions were based on really knowing one white child—that these were words they had heard used by their parents and other adults.

Jean was an unusually intelligent and inventive young woman; she participated in her school system's inservice intergroup education training program. So, after this discussion, she went to the library to locate books like *Swimmy, Sneetches, A Sundae with Judy,* and *Two Is a Team* to read to her class and to use as springboards to discussion about intergroup feelings and attitudes. She used films like *The Toymaker,*[1] and she scoured old magazines for pictures showing interracial cooperation and lack of cooperation. She started a "Junior Peace Corps at Home" and arranged interschool visits with another second grade in another part of the city. She worked intensively with the children's parents and with her staff colleagues to exchange ideas and gain confidence and support. Through these activities Jean reached the conclusion that it was possible to change attitudes if special emphasis and learning experiences were provided early enough. She hoped that her students' next teacher would continue education for attitude change, but she realized, too, that segregation of these children in a ghetto and in a ghetto school had already taken its toll. Schools need more teachers like Jean. She validated what researchers have been finding out for some time—that prejudice exists intragroup as well as intergroup, and that it exists at an early age—probably long before children enter school.

As early as age two-and-one-half, many children are aware of racial differences and begin to associate darker skin color with being "dirty" according to Dr. Kenneth B. Clark,[2] Professor of Psychology of City College of New York. Professor Clark and his

[1] See Chapter 6.
[2] Kenneth B. Clark, *Prejudice and Your Child* (Beacon Press, 1955).

wife studied the attitudes of 253 Negro children, ages three to seven, from a segregated southern school and an integrated northern school. They found that when these children were asked to choose the doll that "looks bad" between a colored and a white doll, fifty-nine percent chose the colored doll. This attitude of rejection of one's own color was further illustrated by the fact that forty-two percent of these children chose the white doll as the "nice doll that looks like you."

In a similar type of study done with 400 young children, ages five to seven, of all races, religions, and nationalities, as part of the Philadelphia Early Childhood Project,[3] the findings revealed that

1. In their conflict situations, specific group labeling appears repeatedly.
2. Children hold fixed notions of other groups and think in stereotypes.
3. Young children are aware of group differences.

Further, these researchers found that among these kindergarten and first-grade children, nine percent expressed open rejection against Catholics, twenty-seven percent against Jews, and sixty-eight percent against Negroes.

By age twelve, behavioral rejection replaces verbal rejection, and at about the fifth grade, the choosing of individuals of other races or ethnic groups as playmates or to sit beside in class disappears. This would help explain why, when desegregation occurs as a result of pressure, and students are put together for the first time when they are preadolescents and adolescents, acts of physical aggression seem more pronounced. These are often blamed on the "mixing of the races," when in reality they are both a part

[3] Helen G. Trager and Marian Radke, "Early Childhood Airs Its Views," Educational Leadership, *Journal of ASCD,* October 1947, Vol. V, No. I, pp. 17–19.

of growing up and a part of intragroup as well as intergroup rejection.

The problem of prejudice, therefore, both in terms of attitude and in terms of behavior, begins *before* children come to school, and continues in growing degree and kind in predictable ways.

Has Traditional Education Changed Attitudes?

It has been widely assumed that the mere acquisition of education as it has been traditionally practiced in our schools will reduce the level of prejudice found in studies ranging from the very young preschool child to various adult religious, ethnic, and cultural groups.

In 1961, Dr. Charles H. Stember,[4] Chairman of the Department of Sociology at Rutgers University, completed a study of the effect of education *per se* on prejudice. He studied the data derived from surveys of the American Institute of Public Opinion (Gallup Poll); surveys by the National Opinion Research Center of the University of Chicago; studies by the Elmer Roper organization; the nationwide study of religion and prejudice conducted by Ben Gaffin Associates; the Cornell Studies on Intergroup Relations; and the series of studies on prejudice conducted by the Opinion Research Corporation. The conclusions of this study include the following statements:

There is little evidence that school consistently causes stereotypes to be rejected, or that the educated are less prejudiced or discrimination-minded in their personal lives. On many issues, the educated show as much prejudice as the less educated, and on some issues they show more.

Dr. Stember finally concludes that merely raising the educational level will not necessarily reduce prejudice against minority

[4] Charles H. Stember, *Education and Attitude Change,* New York Institute of Human Relations Press, 1961.

groups. This does not say that education *cannot be* a powerful force against the development of prejudice, or that it cannot counteract existing prejudices. But it does imply that education, as it has been traditionally understood and practiced, cannot be expected to constitute adequate intergroup education.

The obvious need is for the *appropriate* kinds of education, rather than for the mere increase of the number of years our citizens attend school.

Many teachers were born and educated in the same areas where they now live and teach. With attitudes and values that their cultures inculcated changed little, if any, by education, they continue to teach and judge as they were taught and judged, their attitudes having changed little through their own education.

In one junior high school, paired with another for more equal educational opportunities for interracial groups, such a teacher exhibited her own brand of prejudice and lack of knowledge when she took the first roll call. To each white child she said, "And you were born here, of course"; but of each Negro child she asked, "Were you born in Georgia or South Carolina?" This, in spite of the fact that one young Negro student answered, "No ma'am—I was born in Chicago," and another had lived in the city all of his life in a family whose ancestors were also city dwellers in the teacher's city since before the Civil War!

Another junior high school teacher reported: "Jimmy was such a *nice* boy last year, but he has gone to pieces this year. And only yesterday I saw him walking down the hall with two Negro girls!"

Without sensitivity and without adequate knowledge and preparation, these teachers behaved exactly as the society that produced them expected them to behave. The chances are that these kinds of teachers will do little to change attitudes—they will only perpetuate regional prejudices.

The need for intergroup education to change attitudes, to make use of available knowledge, and to create new attitudes and values with which to refute stereotyping was never more imperative. To gain a proper perspective on the challenge of intergroup education we must have some awareness of the *extent* of prejudice.

The Extent of Prejudice

In recent years there have been many incidents showing the degree of prejudice existing among young adults and adults in the United States. Prejudice carried to its most dangerous and irrational stage caused the murder of three young, unarmed Civil Rights workers in Mississippi during the summer of 1964. Prejudice and bigotry characterize the "far-right" groups represented by the White Knights of the Ku Klux Klan and some other organizations.

In a 1950 poll of 3300 high school students from all regions of the United States, thirty-one percent of the boys and twenty-seven percent of the girls answered "Yes" to the question, "Is the Negro a member of an inferior race?"

As to the extent of anti-Semitism in this country, the findings of the public opinion polls of a cross section of the U.S. put estimates of anti-Semitism at between ten and fifty percent of the population. Allport summarized the extent of American prejudice by estimating that four-fifths of the American population harbor enough antagonism toward minority groups to influence their daily conduct.

A common misunderstanding is that prejudice is a problem of the majority group not shared by minority groups. However, it has been shown in many of the studies that minority groups as well as majority group members have stereotypes about others and about their own groups. Several studies have shown that there is a greater average ethnic prejudice among Negroes than among white people.

One study compared the attitudes of Negro and white college

students, high school students, and adults regarding their willingness to have varying degrees of association with twenty-four different racial, religious, and nationality groups. The study revealed that in each comparison the whites were agreeable to closer association with each of the other groups named than were the Negroes.[5]

Other studies have confirmed the existence of prejudice among Jews, even in the form of anti-Semitism. The problem of prejudice, therefore, is a problem common to all segments of school and community population. The most serious aspect of prejudice is its effect upon the members of those groups toward whom it is directed.

Prejudice is often expressed in discrimination against other groups, in acts of segregation and, in extreme form, in physical attacks against their person and property. Any American who questions the lengths to which prejudiced persons will go needs only to study the repeated incidents of bombing, killing, stoning, defacement of property, and other examples of extreme manifestation of prejudices that have been commonplace during our past history.

Less extreme expressions are exemplified by jokes and name-calling. Needless to say, whatever its expression, prejudice takes a serious toll on the personalities of its victims. The attitudes and behavioral consequences of prejudice on minority-group members have been extensively discussed in the references cited in this section. Sociologists caution that not all behavior of minority-group persons is a result of prejudice or discrimination against them—that much of it is a *consequence* of their social class status. However, aside from social class influences, they indicate that prejudice develops precisely those qualities of behavior that the dominant group dislikes.

[5] J. S. Gray and A. H. Thompson, "The Ethnic Prejudices of Negro and White College Students," *The Journal of Abnormal and Social Psychology,* 1953, 48:311–313.

At the level of attitudes, according to Simpson and Yinger,[6] the expressions of prejudice have the following varieties of consequence on their recipients.

1. Feelings of insecurity, often expressed in hypersensitiveness.
2. Feelings of inferiority often to the extent of *self-hate*.
3. Feelings of superiority, which take the form of increased prejudice, not only toward the dominant group, but also against other minorities and even against members of one's own group.

Distinct kinds of behavior seem to result from attitudes formed because of prejudice. They are:

1. Resignation and passivity, including the lowering of aspirations and motivation, as protection against further frustration.
2. Symbolic status-striving that takes such forms as flashy displays of jewels, clothes, and automobiles; clowning and other forms of exhibitionism.
3. Clannishness.
4. Aggression toward the dominant group, other minorities, and one's own group. Among lower socioeconomic groups this often takes the form of physical aggression.
5. Neuroticism and, in its extreme form, mental illness.

Professor Clark[7] indicated that personality patterns seem to be formed early—by six or seven years of age. In short, the school and the community should provide positive concern and action to promote mental health, to help each student develop his fullest potential, and to improve behavior and attitudes of all young people so that prejudice and its various manifestations can be combated early and continuously.

[6] George E. Simpson and J. Milton Yinger, *Racial and Cultural Minorities: An Analysis of Prejudice and Discrimination* (New York, Harper and Brothers, 1953).
[7] Kenneth B. Clark, *Prejudice and Your Child* (Beacon Press, 1955).

Any program directed at prejudice, whether inside or outside of the school, must begin with an understanding of the *causes* of these antipathies. As for prejudice being inevitable, Simpson and Yinger point out that ". . . it is now universally agreed among scientists that there are no innate antipathies toward the members of different racial, national, religious, or other groups." Sociologists are agreed that prejudice is a product of three basic factors— personality needs, intergroup competitions and conflicts, and culture itself.

Prejudice is first a manifestation of the functional needs of a personality, which is particularly true of persons living in a socially mobile and competitive society such as that of the United States. Where millions are unable to share in the material rewards that every American is allowed to expect, extensive frustration and anxiety are bound to be consequences. Frustration does not always lead to aggression, hostility, or prejudice toward a particular group, but frustration does make people more susceptible to becoming prejudiced.

There are other personality needs served by prejudice as well. Scapegoating, or the projection of one's own failures on someone else, eases the guilt feelings for some of these failures. To *express* feelings of rejection toward members of the "out" group seems to give individuals a stronger sense of belonging and often enhances status within the "in" group. This can be seen in rival "gang" leadership, and in many acts which people might not ordinarily commit were it not for the need to "prove" themselves in the eyes of the group.

To describe the shortcomings of another person seems temporarily to enhance some people's self-esteem, as does the transmission of gossip and rumors. Momentarily they bask in the glow of group attention, and embellish the description more than they had originally intended to. Prejudice and stereotyping may be used in helping the individual to catalogue the endless kinds of situations that he faces in the world, and in helping him to decide "appropriate" responses to these situations. This kind of stereotyping helps the individual to rationalize his attitude and conduct toward members of other groups.

There is both intergroup and interpersonal competition for the economic and political rewards of income, prestige, and power—and this competition is often the impetus for making use of prejudice. In the competition between Oriental and native white Americans in labor crews on the West Coast of the United States, prejudice against the Oriental "newcomers" served the purpose of this kind of conflict. The same kind of strategy can be seen in the struggle between rival politicians in the Deep South, where anti-Negro and pro-segregation pronouncements often appear to be prerequisites to campaigning and to winning elections.

Traditions of culture themselves seem to be equally powerful sources of prejudice. Although a maladjusted, neurotic personality may predispose a person to be prejudiced, a well-adjusted person can be prejudiced, too. As pointed out by Saenger, a well-adjusted person can be expected to exhibit about the same amount of prejudice as his parents and his subculture.[8]

This stems from the fact that every individual is more or less dependent on the approval of members of his culture or primary group for his satisfactions in life. Therefore, if such expressions of prejudice, discrimination, and segregation are considered normal social behavior in the in group, a person can be expected to conform to these practices and prejudices.

An early researcher on prejudice concluded, "Attitudes toward Negroes are now chiefly determined not by *contacts* with Negroes, but by *contact with the prevalent attitude toward Negroes.*"[9] This type of cultural attitude is conveyed by the mere observance of, and participation in, the in-group pattern of discrimination or segregation.

The *power* of this cultural influence is illustrated by the fact

[8] Gerhart Saenger, *The Social Psychology of Prejudice* (New York, Harper and Brothers, 1953).

[9] Eugene L. Horowitz, "Development of Attitudes Toward Negroes," *Archives of Psychology*, No. 194, 1936, pp. 34–35.

that even people with a substantial degree of prejudice have been found willing to participate voluntarily in unsegregated situations when their fellow participants seem to indicate that such participation is appropriate and accepted.[10] *Much prejudice is blind conformity.* It is just so much clinging to prevailing folkways, and does not serve any functional purpose. It is the influence of culture that determines the accepted expression of prejudice, as well as the singling out of groups against whom it is directed.

Effects of Intergroup Contacts

There are many techniques and activities that can be used to combat prejudice and that have proved effective in counteracting prejudice. Many of these will be suggested in later chapters and will be described in concrete and functional terms. However, one particular technique cited by many observers emphasized the important influence of *interpersonal contact* across group lines as an effective *deterrent* to prejudice.

The Cornell University studies of intergroup relations, cited earlier, and involving fourteen *different* research surveys involving about six thousand persons, confirmed the fact that *contact* between individuals of different groups, whether youths or adults, *reduced prejudice in individuals of both minority and majority groups.* Two key studies relating to the effect of intergroup contact also indicate that such contact reduces prejudice whether the contact is voluntary or required by law, court, or administrative decision. This is the best possible argument for taking action *before* group tensions and political overtones have a chance to develop, since integration that is *forced* often takes place under tense and unnatural circumstances.

The first of these two key studies was conducted by the Research Branch of the Army Information and Education Division.

---

[10] John P. Dean and Alex A. Rosen, *A Manual of Intergroup Relations,* University of Chicago Press, 1955, pp. 58–60.

It compared the attitudes of white officers and noncommissioned officers in Europe *before* and *two months after* Negro Americans were first integrated with white companies of soldiers. After two months of integration, which included living, working, and eating together, seventy-seven percent of these officers were more favorably disposed toward Negroes, and none were less favorably disposed toward having Negro soldiers in their companies. In a similar survey of white enlisted men, the Army found that in those divisions with Negro soldiers, only seven percent of the white enlisted men were opposed to the proposal that Negro platoons be brought into their companies. Of the men in divisions with no Negroes, sixty-two percent were opposed to Negroes being brought into their companies.[11]

The second study dealing with the effect of integration on attitudes was concerned with the tenants of public housing projects. Deutsch and Collins[11] studied the changes in attitudes of white tenants toward Negro tenants in two racially integrated public housing projects. They found that the integrated living pattern created "more frequent and more extensive favorable attitudinal change toward Negro people in the project and also toward Negroes in general." Ending segregation in both cases made *interpersonal contact* possible and proved that this could be one of the most effective kinds of *education against prejudice*. When discrimination and segregation are eliminated, we can assume that prejudice will be lessened.

It is important to note that these two studies represent *prolonged* intergroup contacts under circumstances that required cooperation in order to achieve mutual goals and satisfactions. Since our main concern is to utilize those characteristics of intergroup contact that will *lessen* prejudice, it is essential to study those situa-

[11] Arnold M. Rose, *Race, Prejudice, and Discrimination; Readings in Intergroup Relations in the United States* (New York, Alfred A. Knopf, Inc., 1951).

tions where intergroup association can *increase* intergroup hostilities.

There is some available evidence indicating that *casual* contacts are likely to increase rather than decrease prejudice. This seems to happen because persons meeting under casual conditions, with little real interest in moving toward mutual goals and satisfactions, are not likely to have enough contact to counteract the stereotyping that they bring to the situation. Only those traits that tend to confirm individual prejudices are perceived. This is why it is not enough to bring "bodies" together in schools, and then segregate them by academic achievement or by the results of unreliable IQ measurements. In the discussion on grouping, in Chapter 1, the thesis of this book was clearly indicated to be one that recommends more heterogeneous groupings in communities and in school classes.

Additionally, contacts that are laden with tensions or that have been artificially brought about under tension are apt to increase rather than decrease hostile attitudes. We have seen this in the attitudes of parents whose children have been transferred to another school, in the attitudes of teachers who are used to teaching one type of student and have other types placed in their classes, and in the attitudes of students who are already acculturated to their groups' myths of superiority or inferiority.

Concerning the qualities of contact that lessen prejudice, it seems most important to make certain that the getting together is accompanied by mutually motivational and inspirational experiences, and that the resulting associations are pleasant and rewarding experiences. These kinds of contacts serve the purpose of showing minority-group members in roles not usually associated with them, and they help to discourage stereotyping developed through superstitions and folk tales by replacing them with firsthand knowledge.

Recognizing that intergroup association, like any other educational technique, has its limitations and is dependent upon the *quality* of the experiences enjoyed during the association, inter-group contact can be effective in reducing intragroup and inter-group hostilities.

The voices in our society that have said, and still say, "Keep *them* in their places!" and "Why don't *they* go back where they belong?" have no place in a democracy. Certainly people who refuse to change their ways and their behaviors have no place in the schools we need.

Summary

Some clear implications for communities, teachers, and class-rooms of students become evident in the preceding analysis of prejudice. Among the more significant implications are the fol-lowing:

1. Adults are not the only ones who are prejudiced. Children, even of kindergarten age and younger, have begun to de-velop stereotypes and patterns of rejection based on group membership. These patterns are to be found among minority and majority group members in early antipathies, and for these reasons, *intergroup education emphases must begin early* in the school life of children regardless of group status or membership.
2. Traditional education has not proven to be an effective anti-dote for prejudice; as a matter of fact, it has made no dif-ference at all. So *education for attitude change* is necessary.
3. Since personal and group frustrations increase the suscepti-bility to prejudice, every effort should be made to *minimize experiences of frustration and failure* among all groups of students. They need to have a sense of belonging and ac-ceptance in community, classroom, and student groups, and *effort, progress, and contributions need to be praised and rewarded.*

4. Since prejudice is just as often an attribute of the well-adjusted person as it is of the maladjusted person, adults must help children develop *independent habits of respect and appreciation for individual merit*.

5. Prejudice develops, in part, as an attempt to rationalize the *status quo* of discrimination and segregation. Adults have the challenging responsibility of helping young people understand that these are patterns of undemocratic practices rather than evidences of group inferiority or superiority.

6. Any kind of discrimination or segregation makes impossible one of the most effective antidotes to prejudice—*meaningful person-to-person contact across group lines*. Adults, and especially school administrators and teachers, must continually appraise the practices and patterns of student associations to insure that there is no vestige of discrimination or segregation in the community or the school, either in classrooms or in extracurricular activities.

7. Intergroup education cannot exist in a vacuum. It does not develop from books and laws alone, nor does it develop in isolation; rather, it grows in the sunlight of daily contact. Living, working, playing, and studying with people of many ethnic groups provide the *real-life laboratories* of intergroup action, cooperation, and education for democracy.

Opening the doors of our schools and hearts is not enough—we need community-school policies, curricula, and facilities intelligently and creatively designed to meet the needs of modern education. We need alert groups of community policy-makers, Boards of Education, and professionally trained staffs who are attitudinally prepared to treat *every* child with respect and fairness—with love and kindness. We need to support, monetarily and morally, innovations that will permit such staff members to work at the level of their highest competence.

Young people, especially, need opportunities to understand

the distortions of perception that result from ignorance, fear of and separation from others, and the consequences of projecting their own unrecognized and unacknowledged attitudes and traits onto other people. What we know, and what we can learn about prejudice and the antidotes for it, will enable more future citizens to enjoy equal and unlimited personal and group membership opportunities.

CHAPTER 4

GOALS AND METHODS
FOR INTERGROUP EDUCATION

General Definition and Goals for Students

As we have seen through the previous discussions, intergroup education implies much more than just *human relations education*. It is concerned specifically with fostering better relationships among individuals and groups of differing races, religions, national origins, and socioeconomic backgrounds. Furthermore, intergroup education is intimately concerned with the daily lives of each of us throughout this nation and the world, and suggests that we use diversity, as well as similarity, as a catalyst to improved understanding.

Intergroup education is not a course, or a program, or a unit appropriate to only one area of the curriculum or one part of the school day or year. It should permeate every area of community life and school curriculum; for attitudes, values, processes, understandings, and skills that are basic to effective daily functions of children and adults are also basic to the teaching-learning climate of schools.

Emphases in intergroup education are as important for persons of minority groups as they are for majority-group members. Intergroup relations have their geneses in the home life and early school experiences of children, and manifest themselves in young people's behavior, relationships with other human beings, and growing participation in, and commitment to, the democratic way of life.

Therefore, effective school programs for intergroup relations must include well-defined aims and objectives that are valid at all levels of school attainment. There are some common concepts that are appropriate for curriculum planning at all levels.

A. *Attitudes and values*

1. Appreciation of human similarities *and* differences.
2. Utilization of techniques that exemplify the best traditions of true democracy.
3. Respect for equal worth of one's self and every other person.
4. Respect for law and order; honesty and integrity of thought and action; responsibility; and education.
5. Respect for the rights of all to equal protection under the law, as well as equal opportunity to secure education, employment, housing, and equal accommodations.
6. Acceptance by individuals and by groups of the responsibility for protecting human rights and for living up to the obligations of citizenship in a democracy.
7. Acknowledgment that differences denote neither inferiority nor superiority.
8. Acceptance of the value and importance of cultural diversities, and respect and appreciation for the contributions to American life of diverse cultures and religions.
9. Belief in judging others on their individual merits and abilities, without stereotyping because of race, religion, nationality, or socioeconomic status.
10. Belief in cooperating with others to solve common problems, and to improve life for all.

B. *Understandings and skills*

1. Practicing the processes used to carry on democracy—processes such as cooperation, goal-setting, competition, study, work, planning, exchange of ideas, decision-making, and evaluation.

2. Realizing that among members of all racial and cultural groups there are to be found similar needs, desires, feelings, and problems.

3. Accepting the fact that adjustments of behavior and attitudes are often necessary in order to win acceptance by others and promote harmonious living.

4. Being aware that all people are interdependent in fulfilling their needs and solving their problems.

5. Learning to recognize that there is a wide range of physical and mental abilities and talents existing among every racial and ethnic group.

6. Recognizing that differences in attitudes and behavior are determined largely by one's cultural environment, and that they are, therefore, changeable through new kinds of encounters and reactions.

7. Practicing those skills needed to live in democratic societies—leadership, group membership, voting on the basis of qualifications, ability to follow leadership of others when leadership is positive, making wise decisions individually and through group membership, participating in discussion and critical thinking, and providing opportunities to reach consensus and reap the results of good and even poor decisions.

8. Gathering facts from a variety of sources, comparing and weighing evidence, challenging the idea of stereotyping and prejudices, testing superstitions versus reality, recognizing and analyzing propaganda, communicating across group lines, and accepting responsibility for self and others.

9. Learning the art of disagreeing without being disagree-

able, and thinking rationally and objectively about ideas
and people.

10. Avoiding premature conclusions, overgeneralizations, and
stereotyping of people and ideas.

11. Practicing the art of problem-solving by defining problems; gathering and evaluating data objectively; weighing
alternative solutions; selecting best possible solutions and
testing them; evaluating and modifying procedures if
necessary.

12. Being thoroughly familiar with information about facts,
ideas, concepts, successes and failures, future needs, and
general principles of American government and the American way of life.

13. Realizing that laws serve as guides for different people in
different times and places. New times and new needs cause
the creation of new laws, and the modification and
explication of some of the old ones.

14. Maintaining open-mindedness toward ideas, events, and
persons of one's own and differing culture groups.

Goals for American Education

Among the "Goals for Americans" set forth by the President's
Commission on National Goals in 1960, was the following statement:

Vestiges of religious prejudice . . . and, most important, discrimination on the basis of race must be recognized as morally wrong, eco-
nomically wasteful, and in many respects dangerous. In this decade we
must sharply lower these last stubborn barriers.[1]

Various groups of citizens concerned with the welfare of youth
have reiterated their support of intergroup education in schools.
The 1960 White House Conference on Children and Youth,

[1] President's Commission on National Goals, *Goals for Americans, the
Report of the President's Commission on National Goals,* Englewood Cliffs,
Prentice-Hall, Inc., 1960, p. 3.

representing citizens from every walk of life, recommended that
"intergroup education be emphasized in every grade of elementary
and secondary schools."[2]

The importance of intergroup education in schools has been
underscored by the nation's leading professional education groups
for many years. The National Education Association's Commission for the Defense of Democracy through Education reported
to its assembly:

In the opinion of the Commission, the best way to control disharmony
in this country is to educate people in all walks of life to a tolerance
of justices, tensions causing group conflicts, to an understanding and
appreciation of the achievements and problems of racial and religious
groups, and to a respect for the rights of individuals. Public schools
have a distinct obligation in this matter, and a failure to discharge
this obligation will pave the way for great national conflict in the
future.[3]

At this same meeting, the NEA Representative Assembly
adopted the following resolution:

The National Education Association believes that teachers and educational institutions of this country have a heavy responsibility for
educating the youth to understand the achievements and problems
of all groups, and an obligation to develop a determination to remove
the causes of group conflicts.

The National Education Association has maintained a joint
committee with the American Teachers Association to promote
better intercultural understanding and intergroup education. In
1951, these organizations sponsored and distributed, in cooperation with the United States Office of Education, a kit and guide

[2] The American Jewish Committee, "Guidelines Toward Human Rights,
Forum Recommendations of the 1960 White House Conference on Children and Youth." American Jewish Committee, 1961, p. 10.
[3] Commission of the Defense of Democracy through Education, "More
than Tolerance, Suggestions to Teachers on Intergroup Education," Washington, D.C., NEA, 1946, p. 1.

on intergroup education for teacher preparation institutions. In this guide it was asserted that "Intergroup education should be an integral part of every educational program in a democracy."

In implementing the NEA resolution, The National Association of Secondary-School Principals devoted two issues of its *Bulletin* to intergroup education. One, "Curriculum in Intergroup Relations," was published in February of 1949. The other, "Human Relations in Secondary Education," appeared in March of 1955.

In 1960, the NEA's Department of Classroom Teachers and the American Educational Research Association published a booklet on intergroup education as part of its series on "What Research Says to the Teacher."[4] The Association for Supervision and Curriculum Development has long supported education for better human relations. Its Commission on Intergroup Education has distributed kits of materials, cooperated in the development of issues of the ASCD publication, *Educational Leadership,* dealing with intercultural understanding, and fostered many resolutions by the ASCD Annual Conference supporting the extension of intergroup education and democratic human relations.

The American Association of School Administrators also published an administrators' handbook for intergroup education and passed the following resolution: "We commend the work of the schools of the nation in their programs of improving intergroup understanding. We recommend that this work be continued and strengthened. . . ."[5]

The American Council on Education felt the need for intergroup education in schools to be of such importance as to sponsor a four-year Project in Intergroup Education in Cooperating

[4] Jean D. Grambs, "Understanding Intergroup Relation," National Education Association, Washington, D.C., p. 1.
[5] American Association of School Administrators, "From Sea to Shining Sea—Administrators' Handbook for Intergroup Education," NEA, 1947, p. 2.

Schools. It involved 2,500 classroom teachers, school administrators, and community groups throughout the country.[6]

The positions taken by these organizations, statements, and long-term emphases are cited to show that intercultural education is not a current educational fad, but something that many educators and laymen have requested and approved for many years. Their statements and actions have indicated their awareness of the ever-growing importance of intergroup education in our country and in our world.

In spite of policy statements giving sanction to highly controversial teaching techniques and subject matter, Professor Dan W. Dodson points out that "one of education's greatest weaknesses is its inability to close the gap between newcomers who are naive, uneducated, and socially disorganized, and the remainder of the populace in our cities. . . .

"The significance of this problem becomes more apparent when we consider that there are, today, one million more people living in the slums of the cities of America than there are on our farms. It becomes doubly significant when one considers the need for bringing the underdeveloped sections of the world into participation in a space age."[7]

The Role of Educational Administration

A few points need to be made regarding the role of the school administration and policy-makers on the board of education in creating the conditions necessary to implement intergroup education. (Several characteristics of human relations as a curriculum emphasis make the role of the school administrator particularly

[6] Hilda Taba, Elizabeth H. Brady and John T. Robinson, *Intergroup Education in Public Schools,* Washington, D.C., American Council on Education, 1952.
[7] Dan V. Dodson, "Two Position Papers," from *Power as a Dimension of Education,* Center for Human Relations and Community Studies, NYU, N.Y., 1963, p. 1.

important.) Because several characteristics of human relations become part of the curriculum emphasis, the role of the school administrator takes on new dimensions.

First, this aspect of curriculum construction, with its primary concern about changed attitudes and social skills, is relatively new to many teachers. They have never been in situations where they are confronted with either the raw materials or the necessity for planning special kinds of experiences. The school administration, therefore, must assume the responsibility for providing sanction and leadership in the schools, and for cooperating with those engaged in teacher preparation.

Second, there is special need for parental and community understanding of this emphasis, because it is aimed at changing some prevalent and long-standing attitudes and patterns of behavior. Consequently, if teachers are to have a fair chance to carry on intergroup education activities in school, the administrative and policy-making officials must help prepare the way by explaining to the community the need for and the advantages of intergroup education. They must also support the teachers in their attempts to create a favorable climate by encouraging community activity and inservice teacher education.

The starting point of effective intergroup education lies in the active support of the school superintendent and principals. Official policy should be stated clearly by the board of education or superintendent, giving intergroup education a bona fide place in the curriculum emphases of the schools. A concrete step in this direction would be for the superintendent to designate a specific staff member of the school administration to be responsible for the intergroup education program of the school district. Unless someone is responsible for this program, it will quickly be lost in the shuffle of school activity.

In New Haven, Connecticut, for instance, the Board of Education and the Superintendent of Schools, Dr. Laurence G. Paquin, instituted a study of educational quality and racial imbalance.[8] Results of the study caused the Board of Education to "pair" two junior high schools, and to recommend open enrollment in clusters of elementary schools in order to relieve overcrowding and deconcentrate large populations of Negro students. Among the thirteen proposals to promote quality and equality of educational programs was the following:

It is proposed that with the 1964–65 school year, the Board of Education provide budget funds for a series of conferences and workshops for teachers—conferences and workshops designed to improve intercultural and human relations not only in the schools, but in the community.

Such a program was put into effect in September, 1964. Believing that all curricular areas of the school must have a strong foundation of understanding based on intergroup factors, the Director of Curriculum was designated to make this foundation of understanding the focal point of inservice training for teachers during the 1964–65 school year. The Board of Education, the Superintendent of Schools, district directors, K–12 subject supervisors, directors of special programs, community agencies, and principals have been actively involved from the very beginning. The resources from outside of the community were coordinated by Professor Dan W. Dodson, Director of the Center for Human Relations and Community Studies at New York University.

Community-School Relations

Initially, large and small group meetings were held with all principals and supervisors. Following these, conferences were held with all community agencies such as the Council of Churches, Community Progress Incorporated, the Anti-Defamation League, the Human Relations Council, the Urban League, the Jewish

[8] New Haven Board of Education, "Proposals for Promoting Equality of Educational Opportunity and Dealing with the Problems of Racial Imbalance in Schools," June, 1964, New Haven, Conn.

Community Center, United Agencies, and so on. The Parent-Teacher Joint Council was involved in a meeting to discuss concerns of district PTA Units. The city was divided into two large districts with each one having an Intergroup Education Advisory Council, and the weekly inservice meetings combined schools from different parts of the city so that cross-fertilization of staff thinking and current concerns could take place.

Staffs found that although they would have liked more time to prepare for the problems they were facing, they would probably not have known how to prepare previous to the new confrontations. Being in the midst of new and unfamiliar kinds of experiences caused much soul searching and determination to find new ways of doing things. There were quiet interneighborhood Peace Corps at work as each area defined its goals and laid the groundwork for ongoing plans. Civic groups and interfaith and intercultural agencies met with school officials and school staffs to lend their time and talents, and to share mutual concerns, as well as to coordinate parallel community group efforts.

As was to be expected, countergroups with ulterior motives activated themselves. One group banded together to call themselves the "Better Education Committee," wrote letters to the editors of newspapers, organized counteractions against the Board of Education, visited school people on the job, and sent out devious questionnaires designed to get the answers they wanted as well as to play on emotions during difficult times for educators.

New Haven, like other larger cities, is having its growing pains. In New York City, militant parent groups have made school organization for face-to-face intergroup education a national headline issue with school boycotts and bitter recriminations resulting from redistributions of students. Demands are made for a new superintendent and new board of education who will maintain the *status quo,* or who will, so it is thought, "really" represent the people.

The real nature of our changing society and the responsibilities of every American during these times are not generally understood. The withholding of financial support, political overtones, recriminations, and lack of funds to improve education generally are huge stumbling blocks that are difficult to move in municipal governments. But the biggest stumbling blocks are the *attitudes* of various neighborhood groups, and not infrequently of teachers themselves.

Without leadership, financial support, and official sanction, classroom teachers cannot be expected to take many positive steps in issues that are controversial in their communities. Many teachers have been educated in rural colleges and universities, and they need the stimulation and reinforcement of a team approach to the problems and context of intergroup education. Although persuaded of the importance of intercultural education in general, they may not recognize the need for this emphasis in their particular schools.

There are effective techniques which the individual teacher can use to assess the prevalent attitude and behavior patterns in the classroom, but there are aspects of this evaluation that can best be approached on a team basis. An individual teacher, for example, cannot be expected to study the patterns of association of pupils outside the classroom without the sanction of the administration and assistance from teaching colleagues.

Furthermore, since the techniques of intergroup education are relatively new to many of us, we need to share in the wisdom and experience of others who have had more experience in implementing such programs. Such efforts need the competencies of the various academic disciplines, and the full support of the administration.

Area colleges and universities can make students and professors in the various disciplines such as psychology, sociology, anthropology, history, and economics available to school systems for series of interdisciplinary discussion groups. When credit for advanced study and salary increments are offered, incentive and motivation seem to be increased proportionately.

School intergroup education activity will be strengthened by the understanding and participation of parents. In the long run, therefore, involvement of parent representatives, such as delegates to the PTA Joint Council, is important to the healthy survival of intergroup emphasis. Unit chapters of this Council that have developed special interests have been responsible for setting up series of study groups in conjunction with area staffs and neighborhood agencies.

The staff group need not be large or permanent. It must be of working size for each task undertaken. Teachers will be most willing to serve if their participation is on an *ad hoc* basis, if the schedule of meetings is not too formidable, and if released time can be provided for at least part of the work to be undertaken. Since intergroup education is relevant to all facets of the curriculum, *pro tem* committees should include teachers from a variety of grade levels and subject areas. Administration, guidance, and extracurricular programs should also be represented.

Since the attitudes and behavior of students are of primary concern in these programs, the participation of student leaders can be an asset upon occasion. Student councils can make important contributions to the program, as well as other youth groups organized by local out-of-school agencies and churches.

Many communities have agencies with professional staff offering resources and experience that can prove very valuable. In many places, intergroup relations agencies have staff or experienced lay leadership. At the same time we must recognize that the best aid, if unwanted or resented, is a hindrance, not a help. Therefore, at such times and in such ways as the assistance of community organization representatives is desired by school personnel, they should be invited to participate as consultants. If the program is for school personnel, it should stay under the jurisdiction and considered judgment of school personnel.

One of our most serious problems in teacher preparation and recruitment today has to do with adequate preparation for the multitudinous problems of urban teaching. If you are fortunate enough to have a teacher preparation institution nearby, participation by its students and members of its education department can be of valuable assistance on two fronts. Such participation can aid and abet the college's training program, as well as help educate teachers for employment in the school system.

Possible Projects

What kinds of activities could prove helpful for intergroup education committees? There is no blueprint of projects or sequence of steps appropriate to all school systems. An important variable is the degree to which the groups in a given school system are prepared and motivated to undertake intergroup education. However, the following suggestions are based on activities that have proved valuable to school committees with varying degrees of intergroup experience and training:

1. Assess the problems and needs for intergroup education in terms of pupil and teacher attitudes and behaviors. Such evaluation might include
   (a) Conducting a problem census among the faculty and students regarding the state of intergroup relations in the school, and opportunities for staff and students to *practice* intergroup relations.
   (b) Designing and conducting a study of participation, association, and leadership patterns of students from different racial, religious, ethnic, and socioeconomic groups in extracurricular and informal out-of-class activities, as well as cross-grouping within the school.
   (c) Selecting or designing effective instruments for measuring intergroup attitudes, understandings, and skills of students and faculty.

2. Conduct a survey study of intergroup education currently being carried on in each curriculum area of the school, with special reference to new literature and new media for intergroup education.
3. Review the syllabi and curriculum guides of the current school courses to suggest supplementary topics and activities of intergroup content, consistent with the need for a continuity of emphasis and with modern content and media.
4. Organize a school library shelf of effective teaching aids and resources in intergroup education. One area for staff and areas for students will help everyone focus on curriculum enrichment materials and objectives.
5. Provide reading materials on intergroup relations as part of both the formal and informal reading program of students. Public libraries can be helpful in making collections available on an extended loan basis, or in organizing special areas in branch libraries for students.
6. Preview available audiovisual aids in intergroup relations for the purpose of recommending some for classroom use, school purchase, rental, or borrowing. Compile lists of comments, evaluation, and recommended usage.
7. Plan inservice education workshops for teachers on the effective use of intergroup education teaching resources and techniques.
8. Evaluate the school's textbooks regarding their portrayal of minority groups and their contribution to better intergroup relations.
9. Conduct community education activities to create needed support and understanding of the program.

Teacher Orientation

There is no role of the administration more important than facilitating the education of teachers for intergroup education.

Since many teachers have not been exposed to this training in their undergraduate work, there is a special need to provide appropriate education for teachers already in service, as well as those just beginning their careers.

Training is available in the numerous summer workshops in human relations education offered by various colleges and universities throughout the country through the National Conference of Christians and Jews and other intergroup education agencies. Many school administrators offer special incentives to encourage the participation of their teachers in these workshops. Incentives range from salary credit to scholarships.

Other school administrators request teacher preparation colleges nearby to offer graduate-credit inservice courses or workshops in the techniques of intergroup education. Teacher preparation institutions generally stand ready to provide the types of training for which there is expressed demand. Still others arrange after-school workshops to give teachers experience in utilizing effective intergroup education teaching resources and techniques.

In order to encourage teachers to take advantage of these opportunities, certain incentives are essential. It is not reasonable to expect teachers to take time from their other activities unless there is some professional compensation. Such compensation could include credit toward a graduate degree, salary increments, released time from other duties, or payment of the training costs. During the summertime, scholarships that include tuition and subsistence act as strong motivators for enrollment in such courses.

To carry out the plans and projects developed in a workshop, teachers need the support of teaching colleagues and representatives of the school administration who have experienced the same training. Participation by the administration in inservice education activities is vital to success, so it is important that teams of at least two teachers and an administrator from each school participate. Teachers hesitate to believe that the school authorities seriously want real strides made in this direction, if they do not see tangible evidence of the administration's concern.

". . . the torch has been passed to a new generation of Americans . . . unwilling to witness or permit the slow undoing of those human rights to which this nation has always been committed. . . ."

—John F. Kennedy
Inaugural Address
January 20, 1961

Man learns through *all* of his senses.

High School students at American Friends Service Committee Civil
Liberties Conference in California gather to sing in the evening.

No child is born prejudiced.

Much learning is *caught* as well as taught.

"What the best and wisest parent wants for his own child, that must the community want for all of its children."

—John Dewey

There is no role in educational policy-making more important than facilitating the training of teachers for intergroup education.

Antidote for prejudice:
Intergroup contact and association in
cooperative ventures and adventures

The presence of a single school of children from varied racial, cultural, socioeconomic, and religious backgrounds is an important element in the preparation of young people for active participation in the social and political affairs of our democracy.

Activities during and after regular school hours offer unique opportunities for young people to practice the skills of group participation and leadership.

The American Bill of Rights and the Universal Declaration of Human Rights are documents that represent man's age-old quest for freedom and humanity as he struggles to create societies that value human dignity and equal opportunity.

The *degree* of civilization in any culture can be measured by the behavior of its citizens.

The essence of intergroup teaching is initiative and experimentation by each teacher in the classroom; consequently, teachers need the support and backing of administration with respect to their teaching techniques and course content. This is necessary because there are very few textbooks or guides for this educational emphasis. Teachers have no choice but to try new topics and methods of teaching. Such experimentation is bound to result in some "mistakes," and the effects will not be all positive. But the trial and error method at present is the only way to pursue the difficult task of changing attitudes and behavior.

Administrative support is also important in regard to the teaching resources to be used. Textbooks, however much improved, will not be up-to-date in their discussion of intergroup relations concepts and problems. Even while they are being printed, history is being made in these important areas. The daily newspapers may be the school's best teaching ally, and teaching materials and audiovisual materials are available from many non-textbook sources. The Appendix of this book suggests many sources not often investigated or used by schools. The primary needs of teachers are administrative encouragement and provision for creating and using imaginative teaching aids.

Pupil-Teacher Grouping

Administrative support is also needed in relation to teacher groupings and pupil groupings. The effectiveness of any school intergroup education program may be determined by these groupings. A final word needs to be said about this.

More important than what the students hear in the classroom is what they see and experience in the school as a whole. Without the experience of having teachers and classmates from various racial, cultural, and nationality groups, pupils cannot be expected to gain fully the understanding of intergroup education.

Having teachers from minority groups can be of immeasurable value in persuading both majority and minority group students of the sincerity of the school's intergroup relations program. It is of first importance that the Board of Education and superintendents practice a policy of recruiting, employing, and assigning teachers *without* regard to their race, religion, or nationality and *with* regard to special talents and abilities.

Of similar importance are the admission practices of the various curricular and extracurricular programs and activities of the school. If for any reason curricular programs exclude minority-group students, either by barring them from or discouraging them from enrolling, the best intergroup education program will not be taken seriously by students. The job placement practices, and referral activity of the school are equally important, as are the work-study and work-training experiences provided.

And finally, a special word concerning the widespread practice of organizing classes on the basis of homogeneous ability group-ings. It has been observed that ability grouping carried to the extreme can convert racially and socioeconomically integrated schools into racially segregated classroom groups within the same school. Intergroup education cannot succeed without *intergroup association* and *interaction in our classrooms*.

Responsibilities of Teachers

Just as teachers cannot be expected to take radical departures from traditional practices without civic and administrative support, so children will continue to learn the attitudes of their own groups unless teachers take leadership in carrying on intergroup education in classrooms and all-school activities.

Every teacher has the responsibility to carry on intergroup education. Some teachers are new at implementing these concepts; others have carried on activities designed to affect demo-cratic attitudes for years. Certainly, not all teachers will be, or can be, educated to conduct intergroup education to the same depth.

The most important ingredients are the teacher's attitudes and relationships with her pupils. As the psychologist Gerhart Saenger phrased it, "Only the teacher who believes what she teaches can be really effective in reducing prejudice among her pupils. Children are influenced not so much by what is said, but by how it is said. . . ."[9]

Minimum prerequisites for an effective teacher of intergroup education and attitudes are

1. Agreement with the validity of the aims and objectives of intergroup education, especially attitudes that need to be developed among students and colleagues.
2. A strong personal conviction of the value of integrating intergroup education concepts into every teaching activity, even though progress in attitude and behavior change is variable and hard to measure.
3. Rapport with students and other staff members in which free discussion of feelings and emotions, as well as facts, can take place.

Additional preparation in the techniques of intergroup education is always desirable. Working familiarity with the tools of assessing pupil needs and attitudes in intergroup education are particularly needed. These "tools"[10] include

1. Sociometric procedures
2. Participation schedules
3. Social distance scales and other measurements of prejudice
4. Role-playing (sociodrama or psychodrama)
5. Projective techniques

[9] Gerhart Saenger, *The Social Psychology of Prejudice* (New York, Harper and Brothers, 1953), p. 194.

[10] Most of these are described in Hilda Taba, Elizabeth H. Brady, J. T. Robinson and W. E. Vickery, "Diagnosing Human Relations Needs," Washington, D.C., American Council on Education, 1951, 155 pp. H. H. Jennings, "Sociometry in Group Relations: A Manual for Teachers," Washington, D.C., American Council of Education, 1959, 105 pp. R. Cunningham, "Understanding Group Behavior of Boys and Girls" (New York, Bureau of Publications, Teachers College, Columbia University, 1951) 446 pp. H. Harry Giles, *The Integrated Classroom* (New York, Basic Books, Inc., 1959), 338 pp.

6. Pupil diaries and written expression techniques
7. Teacher logs of class procedures
8. Anecdotal recordings of students' informal discussions and reactions

To use these evaluation instruments and interpret their findings intelligently requires supplementary preparation. Fortunately there are at present many institutions and summer workshops where intensive instruction can be secured. Every summer, the National Conference of Christians and Jews, as well as other intergroup agencies in cooperation with colleges, offer credit-granting workshop courses throughout the country for school and community leaders in the whole range of techniques in intergroup education. Inservice workshops are individual educational opportunities for each of us. The school guidance counselor or psychologist might be a valuable resource person for recommended techniques.

Intergroup education is not a challenge beyond the present level of teacher preparation. With the necessary attitudes and convictions each teacher can start where he or she is, and proceed to the depth that background and experience make possible. Advanced education can help and is available for any educator who wants it.

The references used in this book are not intended to be all inclusive, but rather suggested to inspire the reader to investigate some of the fine literature and research available to the scholar on intergroup relations. Teachers have the responsibility to be scholars, as well as to *create* scholars, even long after preservice training is over. Today's world demands that each reeducate himself many times, especially in the areas of current history and its attending implications.

The future lies in the minds, hearts, and actions of those who are being taught now.

CHAPTER 5

DIVERSITY IN SCHOOL CURRICULA

EDUCATION for attitude change requires more than placing bodies in new proximities and associations. The experiences recommended here are just as valid for more privileged schools as they are for the less privileged and more homogeneous schools, for much more than traditional curriculum is implied if new encounters and education for diversity are going to matter.

There are new dimensions of education that add infinitely to possibilities for change. Education is now, at long last, challenged to develop the keys to equal opportunity for all of the children of all of the people. Schools today must do more than transmit the social milieus in which many schools presently operate. These admittedly are fairly well mortgaged to local power structures and value systems. And these social milieus, power structures, and value systems will continue to lock minds and hearts in the Little Rocks, the Prince Edward Counties, the Selmas, and the northern ghettos and suburbs, unless education provides more ways of unlocking human potential.

Appropriate kinds of education implied by these new dimensions can make the real difference. Schools need to find new ways of *integrating diversity* and using the strength and worth that are present in *differences*. For many years, *assimilation* was the keyword and the *melting-pot* idea implied *becoming alike* and *homo-geneous*. Approaches to *integrating diversity* will *use and value heterogeneity* in rich and rewarding educational experiences in schools.

The School That Was, Is, and Can Be

When many people think of schools and teaching, they remember the schools of their youth, and unfortunately, these are the models for too many of our schools today. They are characterized by straight rows of desks that are sometimes securely fastened to the floor; one textbook for each subject with the next "lesson" on the assigned pages; rote-memorization and exact feedback of what had supposedly been learned, or more accurately, pre-digested, spoon-fed, and memorized; rewards for giving it back to the teacher exactly as it was written or said, with demerits for not doing so; all instruction in the classroom with the book and the teacher as the authorities; and homogeneous grouping in homogeneous communities. This is the school that was and, too often, still is.

The *school that was* cannot meet the needs confronting schools today. The mere memorization of lessons does not change one's habits and attitudes. The child from the Ku Klux Klan, anti-Semitic, or Black Muslim home will not change his attitude toward the Catholic, Negro, Oriental, Puerto Rican, Mexican, or Jew simply because a textbook suggests that he accept them as friends. The *curriculum that was* presents little for the modern child to relate to or associate with in his search to bring living and learning closer together.

Today's schools must do more than reflect the attitudes of the society around them, and teachers and administrators must do more than teach and judge as they were taught and judged. New conceptions find movable furniture in classrooms, most often moved about in groups for small group or individual work; many textbooks and other kinds of books with diverse content and viewpoints; teachers who value the unusual or innovative contribution and encourage differing opinions; classrooms that value pupil self-generation and flexibility rather than pre-packaged, static conformity; heterogeneous grouping that allows children to work in and with numerous other children; and multimedia teaching and learning equipment that brings the outside world in, allowing classes to leave the school to visit the outside world.

New conceptions stress behavior for the basis of learning and the true measure of what has actually been learned. Newer methods emphasize the quality of living, building character, and developing attitudes through actual conduct and associations. If we look at the learning process itself as the means, education should hold that everyone, at every age, learns what he lives, and learns his responses as he accepts them and to the degree that he lives them. Gaps between schooling and functioning and chasms between the school and the street need not exist.

From kindergarten through graduate school, integrating diversity into the school curriculum through intergroup education can be a way of life in schools that help students apply what they learn, function well in all situations, and make better use of their talents, aptitudes, and vocations. No one functions in a vacuum or in the world that he imagines. Nor can one bury his head in the sand, and, like the proverbial ostrich, pretend that what he sees and feels is really not there. The world has changed since you started reading this chapter, and it will have changed more by the time you have completed it.

Change itself can be the catalyst for self-renewal in people and in institutions. But attitudes and values are not tricked into change. Teaching them requires the same careful curriculum planning as teaching the other so-called *basics* of a classroom subject or discipline. Teaching requires both the imaginative and creative uses of teaching-learning techniques that help teachers tailor-make curricular and extracurricular learning to the particular needs of each group and each student.

The teaching suggestions here range from topics to questions to activities. They are not intended to be exhaustive, but rather to suggest rich sources of intergroup education teaching techniques and ideas. The sensitive, dedicated teacher will explore other avenues and adapt them to his special needs. This person will let ideas emanate from him and from his students, for a few new ideas will bring other new ideas with them. Audiovisual materials, books, pamphlets, records, and other multiple materials are listed in the source chapter. There are many of these and many fine organizations are willing and are able to help schools locate and use them. Professional staff services are available to any interested school or teacher.

The paucity of materials available through regular school channels has already been mentioned. However, the lack of availability need not deter interested persons from planning a rich program. Generally, teachers have not seen themselves in the business of producing study materials, but have been dependent upon textbook companies to provide what they needed. Unfortunately, what has been included in the books adopted has defined and dictated what would be taught. The day of the single textbook is giving way to the demand for multiple books and media.

The materials used in schools are an important aspect of integrating diversity through curriculum—and these materials must help students *identify with and value differences,* as well as similarities. Perhaps it is time, as is happening in some cities, for educators to give more of their own time and thought and talents to the creation and use of new media and materials. School people might legitimately be accused in many cases of living and teaching as though the Gutenberg Press had just been invented. A meager supply of diluted printed matter, innocuous enough to be bought anywhere, is selected, although not too often by teachers, and is still the only source of learning for many children. There are still boards of education who think that one book for every child in every subject is enough, and who propose school budgets that allow for only part of a book per child per year. By comparison with what is spent on any other aspect of municipal life, educational materials have been at the bottom of the list. In fact, by comparison with what is available in homes and communities, many children find impoverishment in this area when they enter school.

Educators and community policy-makers can no longer avoid the responsibility of providing adequate funds and policies for more—and different—materials than those which dominate so many schoolrooms today. Educators have professional responsibilities too, in conjunction with specialists from many disciplines, to create, develop, and demand more defensible educational media and materials. Nor should vested interests be allowed to dictate what is taught or how it is taught, as schools come to grips with newly enriched cultural and civic environments that provide more effective, and often more undesirable, learning experiences than schools do. To abdicate this responsibility is to sell education short, for history provides many examples of the extinction of societies that developed mass minds from conformity and homogeneity.

As community and school leaders and school staffs plan ahead, they will need to make certain that they use diverse methods and materials, as well as the various important and effective means of communication in today's world. These deserve a place in school programs as schools attempt to implement curricula with broader meanings and purposes than they have been able to do to date.

Operational conditions necessary will include

1. Sharing of financing and support for programs in many kinds of schools in many kinds of communities.
2. Criteria for what is and what is not indoctrination. Indoctrination of single group and subgroup values and qualities has no place in public education. Teaching about and with diversity does.

3. Objectives that include the development of cosmopolitan citizens who can function more effectively in culturally diverse communities, and who are free of racial, religious, regional, or social class provincialism.

4. Opportunities for teachers and students to have the freedom to teach and learn—opportunities that reflect the privilege of these individuals to accept or reject dominant group standards.

5. Well-defined procedures and support for handling controversial issues in classrooms, with assurance that the curriculum provides opportunities for these to be discussed.

6. Development and encouragement of attitudes that open minds to possibilities and foster a climate of experimentation with the privilege of succeeding and continuing, or failing, reevaluating, and trying again.

7. Investigation of more effective ways to regroup children and provide ways for the lower-class child to have new aspirations and inspirations so that upward mobility will be his goal of education, and so that teachers understand intellectually and emotionally that some of the instruments of the middle class need close scrutiny and evaluation.

8. Development of skills and attitudes that will encourage creation of multiple materials and multiple solutions to the myriad new problems which must be faced by instructional practices today.

9. Involvement of many agencies and resources that can help develop skills, materials, and differing emphases.

10. Recognition that there are many kinds of children who learn in many different ways—through all of the senses and through all of their "being"; that curriculum planning must include materials that appeal to eye-minded and ear-minded students, so that different ones can respond acceptably in different ways to different resources and experiences.

Planning Diverse Teaching-Learning Activities

A. *Person-to-person contact*

One of the best preventives of prejudice is the experience of actual association and mutually agreed-upon activities with persons of other cultural groups in pursuit of a common interest. These contacts must be supervised so that the results will be as positive as possible, and so that the associations will be long enough to help each one learn the value of new association and attitudes rather than reinforcing existing ideas of stereotypes and prejudices.

B. *Small group activities*

Cooperative group activities, as contrasted with competitive individual or group activities, provide the best practical experiences in developing wholesome intergroup attitudes and skills. Classroom projects and small research activities will provide students with maximum opportunity to practice the roles of effective and satisfying group learning actions, reactions, and acceptance by classmates. With practice, teachers can develop many techniques for decentralizing the teaching-learning process. Using small groups and committees in classroom planning and management requires special, diversified assignments, recognizing student abilities, interests, and leadership potential. "The next lesson on the next page" given to the entire group is not a defensible curriculum practice.

Community and Student Involvement

A. *Community utilization and study*

School neighborhoods and communities provide a starting place for the study of intergroup relations, but the larger community represented by surrounding areas and complexes provides a learning laboratory not yet well explored by schools or by parents in their excursions with children. This larger laboratory can be used in many different ways, such as the following:

1. *Interviews and talks,* in class and in the community, with representatives of minority groups and community agencies. Different topics can be selected from the ones observed and discussed in local community groups. Parents of children or students from distinct cultural groups can be visited or invited to classrooms to discuss a particular subject.

2. *Field trips* that are organized for specific purposes and are not taken just for the trip. If possible, guides who are familiar with the group or the facility should be secured, and the field trips must be preceded and followed by study and discussion to insure understanding.

3. *Interschool visits* among predominantly different cultural groups are valuable if they are planned around a specific purpose or interest shared by both groups. The idea of *performing* for each other is competitive and unrealistic, although if the sharing involves performing in one way or another that contributes to the mutual interest, this could be considered.

4. *Pooling information and knowledge about community resources* has been done in many different ways, but for the purpose of intergroup education, it should include not only all of the resources available through school staffs, but also those available through intercultural groups, social service groups, and religious agencies. Lists of consultants willing to be contacted may either be categorized and arranged in an intergroup education card file, or mimeographed and given to all staff members. It may be helpful to group people and organizations according to special talents and contributions under headings related to specific units, areas of interest, and subject matter.

B. *Student discussion*

Since attitudes, feelings, and conduct are the primary concerns of integrating diversity into curricula for intergroup education, there is no substitute for frank and open discussion of feelings and facts. Discussion techniques require extra sensitivity and skill to handle, but they are rewarding for teachers and students, since they encourage students to reveal hidden thoughts and feelings and remove the teacher from the traditional role. Some specific techniques include

1. *Using drawings or photographs* that deliberately present "feeling" and "acting" interethnic, interracial visual images. Questions asked to start these discussions can be similar to the following: What does this picture say to you? What do you think these people are talking about? How do you think they feel? Can you tell us more about that? What makes you think so? How do we know? Student discussion and skillful leadership of discussion can give many clues to involvement and investigation.

2. *Role-playing, or sociodrama* through which it is possible to identify oneself with the feelings of others and to practice social skills. There are many fine books about these techniques, and it is important to study them for specific preparation in using role-playing or sociodrama.[1]

3. *Buzz session techniques* are effective, especially in the higher grades. Small, informal groups discuss specific topics, and pupils designated as recorders and reporters relay the key issues and discussion in each session to the entire group later. Again, this is a technique for getting maximum partici-

[1] For instructions, see O. Tarcov, "To Clarify Our Problem; A Guide to Role-Playing," Anti-Defamation League of B'Nai B'rith; G. and F. Shaftel, "Role-Playing the Problem Story, An Approach to Human Relations in the Classroom," National Conference of Christians and Jews; A. Klein, "Role-Playing in Leadership Training and Group Problem Solving," Associated Press, New York, 1956.

pation and expression of thoughts, questions, and opinions. The group can choose the topics cooperatively, or the teacher can assign them.

4. *Story-completion* is another good device. The *NEA Journal* and *Read* magazine for students are two periodicals that have consistently published incomplete episodes of in-school and out-of-school social-perception episodes that present the problem and then ask, "What would you do?" With practice, teachers and students can develop these situations themselves, and the possible solutions or endings suggested encourage diverse thinking and logical analysis of the situation presented. Much can be learned about how students think and what their values are, and they can be helped to see possibilities and solutions other than their own.

5. *News headlines and clippings* can be used in a variety of ways that will be socially sensitizing springboards to discussion, and will reveal hitherto unsuspected knowledge, information or misconceptions.

C. *Other socially sensitizing activities*

Just as the underpinnings of bias are emotional in nature, so the unlearning of bias and the substitution of learning activities that immunize against prejudice and bias must be emotional as well as intellectual. In addition to the preceding activities, the list includes:

1. Using and discussing films that are suggested in the resource chapter (and others like them) that have intergroup education themes and that have appropriate preparation and follow-up.

2. Writing, witnessing, and performing in stage, television, or radio dramas with relevant themes, either developed by students or produced commercially.

3. Reading, writing, or discussing literature that concerns intercultural understanding or misunderstanding. Include

the feelings and problems of persons of different groups, and in terms of different social conditions and pressures.

4. Listening to or participating in the music, rhythms, pageants, and festivals of musicians, artists and other groups from diverse cultural backgrounds.

5. Participating in games and dances from other countries and cultures, or watching demonstrations of these.

6. Selecting and arranging bulletin boards, display cases, and other kinds of exhibits that represent art or artifacts of other countries and races.

7. Observing and learning about religious and cultural celebrations other than one's own. Include celebrations, religious observances, birthday commemorations, and intercultural celebrations such as Brotherhood Week, Human Rights Day, Bill of Rights Day, Columbus Day, Negro History Week, Festivals of Lights, United Nations Week, and Equal Opportunity Day. Make sure that the observance has carry-over beyond the day or the week.

8. Working with parent-school-community groups that meet after school and during the summer to plan intergroup and interneighborhood activities.

9. Planning parent-teacher meetings to solicit help and understanding and to explain what is being done to improve and foster intergroup education.

10. Encouraging colleagues to plan cooperative teaching-learning experiences among themselves, and sharing and pooling ideas that work. Ideas that have not worked well the first time may have other possibilities if shared and analyzed together.

Methods and Materials for Integrating Diversity in Elementary Schools

Elementary schools have numerous advantages in using diversity to highlight intergroup education.

First, of course, is the obviously positive factor of working with children before their prejudices and stereotypes become too firmly established. In light of earlier discussions of well established prejudices existent even before children enter school, it becomes imperative to start as soon as possible. Elementary school children are in formative and inquisitive stages of learning to "be" and "feel" and "think." They are more easily motivated by new and interesting experiences, and they do not have the inhibitions that older students do.

Young children are more apt to express original and unlearned responses, for they have not yet been taught that precocity is not tolerated; as a matter of fact, in young children it is prized. In an older child, the same behavior or comment or observation may be considered impertinence by the adult world.

Elementary schools tend to be smaller, and more out of touch with larger neighborhoods except through television and other media. Therefore it is important to do much more than the traditional neighborhood- or community-worker study. However, the smallness of elementary schools helps the child become known as an individual and not as a member of a large mass. Teachers who teach more than one subject in heterogeneous classrooms are more familiar with accepting children at all levels of achievement and working with more diverse abilities and talents. They also have unusual opportunities to see that experiences in various curriculum areas are complementary to each other and geared to the growth and intellectual development of each student.

During the early, impressionable years of a student's life, he can be taught conformity to the detriment of meaningful living and learning, or he can be taught through the experiences provided by the school that personal identification and individuality are valuable assets. It is here that schools show by example that diversity is valued and fostered in personalities, backgrounds, cultures, and interests. It is here that inner feelings, self-images, and self-respect can be appreciated and encouraged so that when the tension-filled, peer-dominated, and self-conscious years of preadolescence and the teens arrive, these attributes will stand him in good stead. When children arrive at adolescence, these years are immeasurably complicated and confused if deflated self-images and inappropriate education in their homes, communities, and schools have been their lot during earlier years.

It is during the elementary school years that children learn to trust, admire and respect the adults and peers whom they will someday emulate. Teachers set the tone in classrooms and other adults set the tone in homes and in the community. These adults thereby determine whether lessons of citizenship will become a way of life, or whether the words read in books may merely be memorized for the next examination and then forgotten. Adults set the tone for whether activities and conversations are merely ways of passing the time or conscious practice in the skills of diverse and democratic learning and living.

The study of people as members of various groups seems essential from a child's first school experiences in the formal school setting. Because of his limited experiences with persons of many groups, the focus of intergroup education must prepare him both to understand the cultures in which he presently lives and to consider wider and more diverse cultures. Let's start with some possibilities for the language arts and then follow through to some other areas.

A. *Language arts*

Long before a child is able to read for himself what his feelings and his vocabulary have helped him think and say for a long time, parents and teachers should read to and talk with children. These early experiences and impressions are the least forgotten and longest remembered. Communication has many manifestations.

1. Check the "Sources and Resources" section of this book for stories and films that deliberately incorporate intergroup education themes.

2. Use children's questions and comments to help them understand the value of differences and the implications of being different. Sometimes this can be done naturally in the immediate situation, but at other times, it can be remembered and saved to build upon later.

3. In teaching any subject, it is important to use discussion and visual images to counteract stereotyping. Too many beginning reading books, for instance, present the family as an exclusively white unit consisting of a father, mother, and two children who live in a community, generally rural or suburban, of people just like them. Valuing and using diversity implies presenting other realities about families through pictures and through analyzing many kinds of family concepts without passing value judgments. For instance, what *is* a family? There are families with light skins and with dark skins; families with many children and with few children or one child; families with one parent, two parents, no parents, grandparents, or other assorted relatives and dependents. There are families who live in big houses, little houses, shacks, barracks, huts, caves, trailers, apartments, and flats. They live in cities, slums, suburbs, and in rural areas. There are families who are wealthy, who are living on an adequate income, and who are poverty-stricken. Since most study materials do not present family diversity, it is important to improvise so that these classifications are discussed, known, and acceptable concepts and facts of life.

4. The same generalizations are true of neighbors who are all of these things whether they are living in the child's immediate neighborhood or the world's larger neighborhoods. If a child's society and his books teach him that there is only one kind of neighbor—his own—he has little chance of learning that there are other kinds of neighbors and that in today's world these are closer than ever before. A neighbor can be

nearby, farther away, or far away, but today we could reach him or he could reach us in a short time, and today's neighbors have great effect on each other's ways of living, thinking, and behaving, no matter where we live.

5. When freed of adult expectations for perfect handwriting, spelling, and grammar, children dictate and write wonderful continuations of phrases like these:

> A mother is . . .
> A father is . . .
> A family is . . .
> A neighbor is . . .
> A city is . . .
> Growing up is . . .
> Love is . . .
> Happiness is . . .
> Sadness is . . .
> School is . . .
> Teacher is . . . and many more.

6. As children get older, consider these:

   (a) Read to them and have them read biographies, fiction, drama, and poetry that feature feelings, attitudes, and problems of children from different racial and ethnic groups.

   (b) Encourage children to vary their educational and reading diets with books that emphasize both the values and problems of diversity. Include biographies and autobiographies of outstanding persons of diverse origins and religions, especially of groups that are minority groups in our cultures.

   (c) Use folk tales and myths that contribute basic understandings about different people in other times and places, and help children see the reason for the myth compared to the reality.

(d) Help them prepare radio and TV scripts along the lines of "You Were There," and involve them in investigation and research of the attitudes and tenors of the times.

(e) Locate conflicting newspaper and magazine articles on the same incident or subject and help students learn to look at more than one side of an issue. Encourage them to exercise critical thinking through discussing, analyzing, and investigating to form their own opinions.

(f) Assign themes such as:

> How I felt when . . .
> I felt left out when . . .
> Others like (or dislike) me because . . .
> Things I don't like about people are . . .
> I'd like to move because . . .

(g) Have students correspond, by photographs, pictures, or tapes, with children in other parts of this and other countries.

(h) Encourage students to create original stories, poems, plays, and incidents around themes that provide attitude and behavior models and elicit feelings and discussion.

(i) Check the first part of this chapter for interviewing ideas and field trips.

(j) Investigate the origins of words in this and other languages. Compare meanings of words that look and sound similar, as well as words that mean different things in different parts of our own country.

(k) Subscribe to newspapers and magazines from other parts of this country and from other countries. See how different publications handle the same events or issues.

(l) Investigate to see what culture, politics, economics, and geography have had to do with the way various printed versions of events and issues are colored and slanted.

Above all, it should be remembered that the language arts involve speaking, listening, reading and writing; and that, additionally, men communicate in many different ways and through many different media. Important, too, is the evaluation of present materials available and materials recommended for purchase. Check suggested criteria given in the first chapter.

B. *The social sciences*

The social sciences include all of those disciplines that help us to understand who we are, why we behave and live as we do, and serve to help us gradually in bringing logic to bear on feelings, attitudes, and behaviors. Adults recognize these disciplines by the names of geography, history, sociology, philosophy, anthropology, economics, and political science, among others. In the beginning the big ideas within each discipline can be used at each maturity level. It is impossible to work with these generalizations and principles without noting differences as well as similarities and valuing both.

1. Living where we are
    (a) Who are we and where do we live? How do we live and who are our neighbors? *Familiarize* children with the globe as soon as possible, and its large components of land, water, climate, topography, and so forth. Help them *locate themselves* on both the globe and flat maps. Help them *to identify* with both their immediate and larger neighborhoods by mapping routes to school, neighborhoods, schools, shops, nearest cities, and land and water masses. *Include* the school grounds and the interior of the school. *Visit* people like the custodian, school nurse, and the principal, to see where they are and what they do. *Discuss and practice* effective activities for interpersonal relations within the

school and the neighborhood including courtesy and respect for each other, friendliness and friendly curiosity, taking turns and sharing, privileges and responsibilities, facility use, thoughtfulness and consideration for others.

(b) Study different nationality, religious, racial, and socio-economic groups from which students and their neighbors come. Students may be invited to report either on their immediate families and ancestors, or those of someone else. Have the reports include

    I. Value of having many different kinds of people in a community

    II. Countries and areas from which they migrated

    III. Religious and racial origins

    IV. Present and past neighborhoods

    V. Types of living accommodations

    VI. Different languages, customs, religions, food, clothing, and so on

    VII. Work done by various family members and dignity of all kinds of work

    VIII. Recreation, games, music, dancing

(c) Ask questions that will stimulate investigation, thinking, and discussion. Why did families come to that neighborhood? As newcomers, how did they feel? Who helped them feel wanted or unwanted in the new setting? What changes in their ways of living did they make in their new setting? What are basic needs of all people? How do people differ? How do people satisfy the same needs in different ways? Why do people with many similarities tend to settle in the same neighborhoods? Whom do students know from other neighborhoods? How can people from many kinds of neighborhoods and other parts of the country and world know more about each other?

(d) Summarize and categorize elicited responses for the purpose of synthesizing intergroup education concepts.

  I. Most people move for similar reasons, but these can be grouped in many ways such as better jobs, better housing, more educational opportunities, family considerations, more freedom, and so forth.

  II. The majority of people experience the same feelings and problems as newcomers, but some have more problems than others for various reasons.

  III. Members of many groups have had to make certain adjustments in their ways of living to gain acceptance in new communities, and many community members have changed their attitudes about certain kinds of people when they really knew them as neighbors and friends.

  IV. People satisfy the same needs in an endless variety of ways, even within the same groups. For them, these are the best ways even though they might not seem best to someone else.

  V. All groups have made valuable contributions to communities, the country, and the world.

  VI. We share responsibilities to help newcomers, understand ourselves and others better, and to improve our own and other communities.

  VII. Location, climate, work available, and the type of community affect the way people think and act. Differences, as well as similarities, are important and valued.

2. Workers in our own and other communities

 (a) Study representative samples of kinds of work done by people in the immediate community that benefit the families represented in the class.

 (b) Discuss why we are dependent on other communities

all over the world for those goods and services that are not available in the immediate community.

(c) List those things that are needed that are and are not available in the immediate community.

(d) Collect clippings, pictures, advertisements, and news items about work in both the immediate community and other parts of the country and world.

(e) Visit industries and shops in the immediate and larger neighborhoods.

(f) Visit parents and relatives on-the-job and discuss the importance of their work.

(g) Investigate community services and agencies, what they do, and how they serve.

(h) Develop understandings that

    I. People have many kinds of talents, interests, vocations, and avocations.

    II. Persons in all kinds of work perform valuable, needed services.

    III. It is the quality of the service, not job status, that is important.

    IV. Education helps people get better jobs and jobs they might like better.

    V. There are many new kinds of jobs that require special training.

    VI. There is now, and has been, job discrimination.

    VII. Many people who are unemployed do not have the education or skills necessary for the jobs that are available.

    VIII. Persons of all occupational groups deserve respect and appreciation for their contributions to our welfare.

3. Living where others live

(a) From the earliest grades, children can understand some kinds of aspects of living in other places. The main criteria is that the picture of other parts of the country or world not be a stereotyped one such as presenting Eskimos in igloos, Indians in tepees, and Africans in jungles or caves. There is a great need for teaching materials that will do these jobs, but teachers who will become students themselves can ferret out accurate information and translate it into good learning experiences for children.

(b) Select at each grade level different parts of the country or world to study in depth, but use current events, children's backgrounds and new interests to investigate any area at any time.

(c) Locate the area being studied, and relate to students' own locations in as many ways as possible, helping them understand similarities and differences. Investigate climate, predominating culture patterns, and ways of living.

(d) Utilize many media to bring the world to the classroom. Preview all materials to be used, since many are inaccurate and stereotyped. If you know this, it can be used as a valuable teaching tool by drawing attention to misinformation, omissions, and inaccuracies.

(e) See how culture, climate, housing, and work have affected lives of others.

(f) Investigate schooling and education, determine problems and possible solutions.

(g) Recommend television documentaries for home viewing, and supplemental reading from nearby libraries.

(h) Develop individual and small group techniques for investigating other world cultures, languages, customs, religions, art, music, entertainment and festivals.

(i) Investigate the production, exchange, distribution, and consumption of goods and services to and from that section and other parts of the world, including the student's own area.

(j) Investigate history and contributions of members of different faiths, races, and cultures, including why they came (or left), where they settled, problems they met, present-day status and conflicts of various groups, leaders that emerged, etc.

(k) Investigate materials from various sources such as your State Civil Rights, or Human Relations Commission; travel agencies; libraries; various agencies and associations; businesses; chambers of commerce; embassies, State Department of Education, curriculum materials centers, the United Nations, publishing companies, national interfaith and intercultural agencies. (Lists of some of these materials and agencies are available in the last chapter.)

4. Study the need for and development of world and local organizations like

The United Nations
international trade organizations
international communications systems
social and family organizations
Friends Service Committee
councils of churches
local and national governments

The League of Nations
international transportation organizations
Jewish community councils
Anti-Defamation League
National Association for Advancement of Colored People and Committee on Racial Equality
juvenile and other courts
United Nations Educational, Scientific, and Cultural Organization and United Nations Children's Fund

Find out also what countergroups there are, how each group handles current issues, what their beliefs are, and how they solicit membership. Help children think critically about the purposes and functions of groups.

5. Older children, especially by the fourth, fifth, and sixth grades (and particularly if they have background just described for younger children) can gain rich understanding from studies like these:

   (a) Characteristics of early religions and civilizations, including those that have lasted into this era and the ones that did not survive.

   (b) Ancient faiths of the Babylonians, Egyptians, and Greeks, as well as civilizations such as the Mayan and Incan.

   (c) Their roles in art, architecture, mathematics, sculpture, business, science, and literature. How have they affected life today?

   (d) What were the possible reasons for the decline and fall of the civilizations they represented?

   (e) Economic bases of wars, slavery, sweatshops, labor unions, and indentured servants and workers.

   (f) Illustrations of the rich diversity of American life and contributions of many peoples in many fields.

   (g) Investigation of stereotyping or "slanting" content of books and other media in such ways as to be unfair to various religious and ethnic groups. Examples might include treatment of Negro and Indian Americans, treatment of Jews and Nazi persecution of Jews, treatment of immigrant groups, immigration law discrimination, policies relating to displaced persons of our own and other countries, and stereotyping like the following:

       i. The Asiatic immigrant as a strange, unassimilable outsider

     II. The Negro as a naturally dull, backward, lazy, un-
        trustworthy person
     III. The American Indian as a decadent savage who is
        all but extinct
     IV. The Italian as a mobster or gangster
     V. Other stereotypes

C. *Science and mathematics*

1. Plan studies that involve the causes of physical differences among racial and ethnic groups. Include myths, scientific evidence, social-biological-physical sciences that have contributed to man's knowledge of man, as well as scientists from many backgrounds and cultures.

2. Investigate the ways that all people and civilizations in different times and places have built on accumulated evidence and experimentation of those before them to accumulate the knowledge and technology we have today. Encourage children to think of new possibilities and needs, such as population growth and what it will mean for every aspect of science and living.

3. Investigate scientific and mathematical contributions of early civilizations such as the Mayas and Incas, and the reasons for extinction of these civilizations.

4. Study the history of diseases that have killed and maimed mankind, the superstitions and practices connected with early "medicine," development of control and immunization against certain diseases, and ethnic origins of scientists who contributed.

5. Examine similarities and differences among all persons of the human race, and list scientific bases for similarities and differences.

6. Around themes such as astronomy, astrology, rocketry, space exploration, and disease control, note the variety of

scientists and mathematicians (often the same people), their racial and ethnic origins, and the temper and knowledge level of the times in which they lived and worked.

7. Study the variety of systems of weights, measures, and money, past and present.

8. Investigate climatic, seasonal, and universal effects upon human beings, as well as the causes and uses of the calculations of these phenomena.

9. Investigate ways people earn, spend, and save money; study early barter systems and learn whether any exist today.

10. Trace the history of various monies and media of exchange.

11. Investigate and graph population trends, the growth of cities, the disappearance of small towns and farms, ethnic groups' removals and replacements, population decreases, factory and business removals, and population projection.

12. Discuss the implications for health, food, work, homes, and so forth.

13. See what oceanography has to offer for helping solve future problems.

14. Study and graph incomes of ethnic groups in the local community and elsewhere. Use information from the Department of Health, Education, and Welfare to compare these.

15. Learn what possible career opportunities will be opening through mathematics and science.

D. *The arts*

1. Music

   (a) Sing songs and listen to music that represents expressions of people in different times and places. Include folk songs, work songs, ballads, pop music. Find out when and where they were written, and learn about

the composers or groups from which they emanated.
Learn some of them in the native tongue or dialect.

(b) Listen to recordings of music of various ethnic groups
authentically performed, and study different and
unique musical instruments and scales of music used
to get unusual or unfamiliar effects.

(c) Study the cultural origins of various musical instruments, types of music. Arrange to attend concerts, folk
festivals, ethnic group musicals, and musical dramas
representing various ethnic groups.

2. Art education

(a) In connection with other cultures and nationalities,
arrange for exhibits from museums, art organizations,
galleries, students' families. Better still, if possible,
take children *to* the exhibits. Exhibits can include
dolls, artifacts, sculpture, paintings, carvings, em-
broidery, models and pictures of architecture, photographs and information about festivals and observances, religious symbols, and so forth.

(b) Study the origin, development, and significance of
these to the culture they represent and to our own cultures.

(c) Investigate different media and materials people have
used to express themselves artistically and creatively
in different times and in different places.

(d) Make posters, draw, or paint pictures illustrative of
intergroup themes.

(e) Exchange drawings and paintings with students in another part of the country or of the world.

(f) Use films and trips to art galleries and museums as
springboards to the world of art appreciation and
understanding and appreciation of other world people.

(g) Invite people with special talents to talk with the class, or to involve the class in a special project such as silk screening, blocking, sculpture, weaving, painting.

E. *Health and physical education*

1. Check some suggestions under Science and Mathematics.
2. Investigate sites of Olympic Games, origins and contributions of participants, and records of achievements.
3. Practice good human relations in choosing team leaders, playmates, and in organizing teams.
4. Develop good personal habits of health, cleanliness, posture, grooming, eating habits, weight control.
5. Investigate recreation areas, playground facilities, kinds of recreation.

Methods and Materials for Integrating Diversity in Secondary Schools

Schools today are being reorganized in various ways. Traditional "grade" lines are being erased, and different age groupings are being placed in new associations. Some of the older plans being revised include those known as 3–3–3–3, 6–3–3, 8–4, and 4–4–4. Here, the term "secondary" is used to include the middle and upper schools where traditionally there has been one teacher for each subject and students rotated to each on a regular, evenly spaced schedule. Some new combinations of *modular scheduling* (longer and shorter periods of time based on needs), *large-group, small-group* and *individual conferring, core curriculum* (the problem-centered curricular development which permits several subject areas to focus on the same area simultaneously), and *team teaching* (which utilizes many teacher talents and personalities to teach the same groups of children) may help us synthesize teaching-learning experiences for teachers and children.

Here, as in the elementary school, community policy makers, educational administrators, curriculum specialists, and college and public school teachers need to investigate both the validity of what is being taught in today's changing world and the quality of learning experiences for students of all ages. The world has an unprecedented need for people who help themselves and others learn *how* to think—not *what* to think.

John Gardner[2] sheds some light on qualities needed when he says:

> If we indoctrinate the young person in an elaborate set of beliefs, we are ensuring his early obsolescence. The alternative is to develop skills, attitudes, habits of mind, and the kinds of knowledge and understanding that will be the instruments of continuous growth and change. Too often, we are giving our young people *cut flowers* when we should be teaching them to *grow their own plants*. We are stuffing their heads with the product of earlier innovations rather than teaching them how to innovate. We think of the mind as a storehouse to be filled when we should think of it as an instrument to be used.

In this same book, Mr. Gardner discusses the problem of building a vigorous and creative culture, capable of adapting to change, of getting itself out of its own rut, of avoiding the decay and decline that befell the Roman Empire and other civilizations before and since, and he says that the most effective means of building and maintaining such a society is through education that fosters versatility. Versatility, he contends, means "giving increasing emphasis . . . to instruction in *methods of analysis* and *modes of attack* on problems . . . more attention to basic principles, less to applications of immediate 'practical use.' . . . It means teaching habits of mind that will be useful in new situations—*curiosity, open-mindedness, objectivity, respect for evidence,* and the *capacity to think critically.*"

In our middle and upper schools, especially, we need groups of teachers who will be competent not only in their own fields of specialization, but also interested in their colleagues' fields of

[2] John W. Gardner, *Self-Renewal: The Individual and the Innovating Society* (New York, Harper & Row, 1960).

specialization and modes of inquiry. Together, such teachers can create dynamic learning experiences for and with students as they cross-fertilize each other's ideas for their students and the curriculum. The teaching tools and techniques of the "school that was," described earlier in this book, will not do for the "school that can be" or the schools we need today and in the future.

The attitudes, habits, feelings, associations, and actions of adults are qualities that affect the lives and learning of youngsters more than any of us realizes. Inflexible, rigid, closed, dogmatic, prejudiced adults have created today's dilemmas. May the schools and societies of the future be the instruments for resolving these dilemmas, opening minds to things possible, and moving forward.

The suggestions which follow are grouped by subject, but suggestions are also given and implied for all teachers to consult areas other than their own, as well as their own. Test models will be the trial balloons which should inspire all of us to dare new attempts.

A. *English*

Our world is one of communication. Language—heard, spoken, written, and read—is the important element of English, as well as other languages. English programs for modern schools will need to give equal attention to speaking, listening, writing, and reading as the skills students will need in order to communicate effectively at any age and in any area.

Mass media communication is a relatively new phenomena in our society, especially with the increasing availability of television to all. We are just beginning to understand the implications of having millions see the same events as they are happening, hear the same speeches, news, and commercials, know the same popular musicians and music, and be exposed to the same educational media whether selective or not. Through use of modern media in school programs, we can accomplish a number of intergroup educational goals; and we can help develop more critical and more perceptive citizens through understanding and using modern mass communication media experiences both in and outside of school. For instance:

1. Place on a bulletin board pictures that have to do with characteristics of citizens of the United States. Ask questions about them; for example:

    (a) This is a bulletin board that shows some characteristics of citizens of the United States. What are your impressions?

    (b) What do these pictures suggest to you? Is this a true picture?

    (c) Is it representative of all of our citizens? Why not? Have we failed to include anything?

    (d) If you were a citizen of a foreign country, what impressions of an American would you get from these pictures?

    (e) Can you list what you think should be included?

    (f) If you were to write on the subject "What is an American?" what would you write?

2. Have students plan, collect, and display a more composite picture of the "American" by making a new bulletin board. If representatives of minority groups, multiracial and multiethnic people in many occupations and activities, or current problems being discussed in newspapers and periodicals fail to be represented, ask questions that will stimulate their inclusion and consideration.

    (a) Encourage free discussion and writing. The teacher's role here is to foster the climate in which real feelings and impressions can be brought into the open. Learn to ask the kind of question that "goes somewhere"— that does not require the pat answer—that stimulates more thinking and debate. These experiences are a legitimate part of the English curriculum.

(b) Change the picture or headline center frequently, and use new themes such as liberty, equal opportunity, democracy, housing, occupations, education, recreation, etc.

(c) Mimeograph a copy of a newspaper clipping that features a current community debate or local, national, or international social concern, or put it on a transparency and use with an overhead projector.

(d) Read and discuss it with the class. If teacher and students are in a rural or suburban area, discuss the characteristics of the city, if a city is involved, as compared with your own area. If you are living and teaching in a city, get student impressions of this article. Do they believe this is true? Why? Why not? Is this true for any other groups now? In the past were there such problems and groups?

(e) Discuss the headline. Does it represent the article? Could students write another one that would be better? What about the first paragraph? Does it make you want to read further? Why? What has the writer done to encourage his reader to read beyond the first paragraph?

(f) Discuss placement of the article in the newspaper or magazine. How prominent was the article?

(g) How many kinds of problems did the writer or speaker discuss? Do you think the newspaper article was written fairly?

(h) Suggest that students look for other articles on these same kinds of problems as a homework assignment. List television programs and newscasts that might be used outside of school hours to hear other opinions and viewpoints on these problems.

(i) Practice writing headlines, lead paragraphs, and news articles about specific aspects of the problems mentioned.

    (j) Assign individual or group reading or viewing assignments in connection with concerns of this and other articles.

    (k) Organize class in small groups to discuss and plan ways they might learn more about these problems. Help them to decide modes of inquiry, set up interviews, formulate questions, and report orally or in writing about their investigations and personal interviews. Community welfare and social agencies, as well as civic planning and redevelopment agencies, are excellent human resources. So are many ministers, priests, and rabbis. Most would be willing to visit the classroom as well.

3. Use tape recordings and records.

    (a) In selecting recordings of famous speeches, make certain that they are understandable—well read or spoken by either the author or some other highly competent speaker. The same is true for famous works in literature, drama, or music that will lend depth or credence to ideas.

    (b) Use great documents such as the Gettysburg Address, Preamble to the Constitution, Bill of Rights, Bill of Human Rights, F. D. Roosevelt's Second Inaugural Address, Presidential Oath of Office, Roosevelt's Four Freedoms Address, Kennedy's Inaugural Address, Washington's Farewell Address, and Lincoln's Second Inaugural Address. Read the message written on the base of the Statue of Liberty.

    (c) Encourage students to read and record all or parts of these documents. Have them listen to themselves as they sound to others.

    (d) Make lists of words and phrases such as *created, equal, unalienable, rights, pursuit of happiness, governments, instituted, just powers, consent of the governed, con-*

ceived in liberty, dedicated, proposition, union, domestic, tranquility, liberty, posterity, respecting religion, convert, retreat, wretched, teeming, homeless, "tempesttost," etc. Investigate their possible meanings, and then their meanings in the context of speeches and documents studied.

(e) Assign theme topics such as

Americans are status conscious.	Americans are materialistic.
Americans love their children.	Americans love all children.
Americans are competitive.	Americans are prejudiced.
Americans are progressive.	Americans' use of leisure time.

Suggest that students may develop the topic either pro or con, but that they must substantiate their opinions.

4. Read biographies, fiction, drama.

(a) Classroom experiences of over a thousand teachers involved in the American Council on Education's Project in Intergroup Education in Cooperating Schools, indicated that biographies, fiction, and drama offer valuable vehicles for sensitizing students to the feelings, attitudes, and problems of representatives of different cultural groups, and for creating respect and understanding for the differences.[3] Some of their suggested themes around which to build reading, drama, and discussion are:

Patterns of family life.

Community contrasts.

---

[3] For this annotated list of 650 books for children's reading see Margaret M. Heaton and Helen B. Lewis, "Reading Ladders for Human Relations, Revised and Enlarged Edition," Washington, D.C., American Council on Education, 1955, pp. 7–8. Regarding this use of literature, see also Staff of Intergroup Education in Cooperating Schools, "Literature for Human Understanding," Washington, D.C., American Council on Education, 1948.

Economic differences.
Adjustment to new places and situations.
Belonging to groups.
Experiences of acceptance and rejection.

(b) Learn the distinguishing characteristics of facts, fiction, opinions, rumors, and generalizations, as applied to thinking about people.

(c) Have students suggest statements they consider to be facts. Discuss which portions of submitted statements are fact, and which are opinion, as well as why.

(d) Have students write descriptions of a trait which they think is peculiar to members of a racial, religious, nationality, or socioeconomic group. Then assign each one to do research on his own writing or on a classmate's composition, and then write an evaluation of its accuracy. Discuss written evaluations.

(e) Discuss the nature of prejudiced remarks, the effect of "labeling" on attitudes, and some of the ways one might effectively respond to them.

(f) Read selections reflecting various literary styles which are characteristic or originated from other countries; e.g., the hokku and Tonka of Japan, terza rima of Italy, the mood of the Irish short story, the allegory of South Africa, the origin and nature of folk tales.

(g) Investigate ethnic backgrounds of authors of favorite drama, poetry, fiction, autobiography, etc. Read accounts of their youth, times, and problems.

(h) Develop TV programs or radio dialogues based on such actual programs as "You Were There," "Twenty Questions," "To Tell The Truth," "What's My Line?" and others.

(i) Work with music, art, and social science teachers to provide other kinds of experiences in listening, speaking,

investigating, reading, writing, understanding, and appreciating. Your staff colleagues are often your best
resource persons; they may know of others with special
collections or competencies.

B. *The social sciences*

If some of the kinds of experiences suggested under *English*
sound like social science curricula, this is intentional. The lines of
distinction are not as marked as some of us would make them, and
the most important thing a staff could do would be to cross these
traditional boundaries so that curriculum for today's students would
function for them like a well-constructed mobile—in perfect harmony and tune with their learning experiences and the adults in
their schools. Provincial and traditional chasms can be bridged
in many ways by those willing to try. The reader who specializes
in the social sciences is therefore referred to the curriculum section
under *English*.

1. Economics

In 1960, the following article appeared in the *Philadelphia
Inquirer:* [4]

Suppose in our imagination, we could compress the total population of the world, more than 2½ billion people into one town of
1000 people.
    Dr. Henry Smith Leiper, a leader in Congregational churches
and in the American Bible Society, has done just that. This image
of the world is graphic.
    In this imaginary town—the world reduced in exact proportion
to a community of 1000, there would be sixty Americans. The
remainder of the world would be represented by 940 persons.
    The sixty Americans would receive half of the income of the
entire town, with the other 940 dividing up among the other half.
    About 330 in the town would be classified as Christians, and

[4] Jack Mably, "How U.S. 'Appears' in One-Town World," *Philadelphia
Inquirer,* May 24, 1964.

670 would not be so classified. Fewer than 100 would be Protestants, and some 230 would be Roman Catholics.

At least eighty townspeople would be practicing Communists and 370 others would be under Communist domination.

White people would total 303, with 697 nonwhite.

The sixty Americans would have an average life expectancy of seventy years; the other 940, less than forty years average.

The sixty Americans would have fifteen times as many possessions per person as all the rest of the world.

The Americans would produce sixteen percent of the town's total food supply. Although they'd eat seventy-two percent above the maximum food requirements, they would either eat most of what they grew, or store it for their own further use, at enormous cost.

Inasmuch as most of the 940 non-Americans in the town would be hungry, the disparity in the food supply might understandably lead to some ill feeling among the townspeople.

The Americans also would enjoy a disproportionate share of electric power, coal, fuel, steel and general equipment.

The lowest income group among the sixty Americans would be much better off than the average of the rest of the town.

Half of the 1000 people would never have heard of Jesus Christ and what He taught. On the other hand, more than half would be hearing about Karl Marx, Lenin, Stalin, and Khrushchev.

(a) Mimeograph this selection or put it on a transparency and use an overhead projector. Read orally with the class.

(b) Since economics is a study of the production, exchange, distribution, and consumption of goods, use an article like this to find out what your students' understandings of these terms are. You will find many misconceptions.

(c) Discuss terms like "minority" and "majority" groups. What do these terms mean in our own communities, our state and country, and in the world? Does the meaning change in the context of the article just read?

(d) Within our own communities and country, compare the

standards of living of minority with majority groups. Bring out the fact that in many sections of our own country such as Appalachia and some large cities, the majority group may be what some people would consider the minority group.

(e) Compare the standards of living among minority and majority group members in a given section of the country. Divide the class into small groups for investigating and reporting on different sections of the country that have been selected. Include Alaska, Hawaii, cities, suburbs, and both thriving and depleted rural sections. Include also the tenant farmer, the migrant worker, and the unskilled laborer.

(f) Investigate the effects of discriminatory educational and employment practices on the economic status of minority groups. (Many state Human Relations Commissions, and Boards of Fair Employment Practices can supply you with facts and figures.)

(g) Analyze the financial costs of discrimination and segregation.

(h) Investigate regional projects where large-scale physical and human renewal projects are in process.

(i) Study the economic causes of discrimination, segregation, and scapegoating.

(j) Study the changing occupation patterns of our national minority group citizens. Analyze their status in labor unions.

(k) Discuss the cost of slums to a community; analyze the cost of unemployment and family relief payments.

(l) Review the migration and employment status of minority group workers in relation to industrialization; depressions and recessions; the Civil War, and World Wars I and II; automation.

2. United States History
    (a) Study the people of America and where they came from.
        If your community has a variety of persons from di-
        vergent ethnic backgrounds, apply the same criteria to
        studying about them. Include immigrants, migrants, pil-
        grims, slaves, and displaced persons. (Consult conflict-
        ing sources.)

    Where they came from   Problems between first-
    Their religions and races   and   second-generation
    Reasons for migrating   immigrants
    Where they settled   Contributions to this
    What their migratory   country and community
        patterns were   Reality and popular
    Problems encountered   stereotypes
    Migratory patterns of   Confinement of American
        persons they displaced   Indians to reservations,
    Present status and prob-   Japanese-Americans
        lems   during World War II,
                                      etc.

    (b) Evaluate contrasting theories of Americanization:
        "Melting pot"
        Cultural pluralism
        Minority-majority
        Cultural democracy—e.g., loyalty to democratic values
            plus maintenance of cultural variations.
        Discuss to what extent people should live according to
            native customs, and to what extent they should con-
            form to American ideals and traditions.
    (c) Examine our immigration laws and policies as to their
        provisions, reasons for passing and their effects, in-
        cluding the Alien and Sedition, and the McCarran Acts.
        Study recent recommendations and reasons for them.
    (d) Discuss the historical development and meaning of the

American documents mentioned earlier under *English*. Include also the United States Supreme Court decision on segregated schools, and the Preamble to the UNESCO Constitution, as well as the Universal Declaration of Human Rights.

(e) List the contributions of various religions, and discuss the reasons why this country has a Judaic-Christian heritage.

(f) Investigate and list the contributions of many religions, as well as of persons of divergent religious background. Visit art galleries, museums, industrial institutes, and concerts. Use recordings, films, biographies, TV and radio, newspapers and periodicals including *Ebony* and the *New Republic*.

(g) Review the history of religious and ethnic intolerance and conflict:

Anti-Catholicism	Oppression of Protestants and
Anti-Semitism	other groups and sects

(h) Examine the history of majority-group treatment of minority groups such as American Indians, Negro Americans, Orientals, immigrants and their children, aliens, Americans with origins from countries hostile to the United States, Mexican-Americans, Cubans, Puerto Ricans, religious groups, etc.

(i) Study minority-group movements, such as Zionism, the Garvey Movement, and the Southern Christian Leadership Conference. The kinds of issues being considered by the World Council of Churches and the Ecumenical Council in Rome reflect contributions that can be made by the world's religious groups.

(j) Survey the development of laws that both aid and thwart the implementation of human rights principles. Discuss States Rights and Federal Rights as they presently exist.

(k) Examine the voting-rights history of all Americans. Include study of the Poll Tax, "White Primary," "Grandfather Clauses," Women Suffrage, violence and intimidation, voter-registration drives, Domestic Peace Corps, property-educational-"character" requirements.

(l) Review the history of law enforcement and court justice regarding minority groups, including different social classes. Use a current concern such as the murder of three civil rights workers in Mississippi, and numerous other miscarriages of justice in similar cases. Investigate jury selection, and the basis for our system of court procedure at the local, state, and national level. Consider what recourses there are.

(m) Investigate the history of bigoted groups; e.g., Ku Klux Klan, Know-Nothing Party, American Protective Association, John Birch Society, etc.

(n) Investigate the "slant" of news reporting, the characteristics of political maneuvering, the viewpoints of extreme "right" and "left" groups.

(o) Take one ethnic group such as the American Indians, and follow their moves and removals to the reservation. What laws and what attitudes caused the situations in which these groups find themselves today? What are the responsibilities of all Americans to the First Americans? Are there analogies among treatments of other groups? What are the elements in society which have relegated some Americans to second-class citizenry?

(p) What were the contributions of American Negroes during the Civil War, and other great wars in which their country has been involved?

3. Civics

Appraise the role played by government in these times regarding Civil Rights:

(a) Voting rights
U.S. Constitution
State voting restrictions
Court decisions

U.S. Departments of Health,
Education, and Welfare
U.S. Commission on Civil
Rights
U.S. Department of Justice

(b) School desegregation and integration, including
1954 U.S. Supreme Court decision
Recommendations and practices in your area and state
Southern state governments versus the courts
Northern and southern communities versus the courts

(c) Fair employment practices
State fair employment practice
Federal fair employment practice, executive orders, and
committees.
For instance:
President Franklin Roosevelt's Committee on Fair
Employment Practice; President Truman's Executive
Order on nondiscrimination in hiring; President's
[Eisenhower] Committee on Government Contracts;
President's [Eisenhower] Committee on Government
Employment Policy; President Kennedy's Committee
on Equal Employment Opportunity

(d) Fair housing practices
Supreme Court decisions on restrictive covenants
Recent legislation in California (1964 elections)
Federal housing agency policies
Fair housing practice laws and ordinances

(e) Equal opportunity to use public accommodations
Federal Court decisions
Incidents involving efforts to force lawful accommodation
Examples of refusal to comply and ways of "getting
around" the Civil Rights Law

Human Relations Acts (contact your state Human
Relations group)

Fair educational practices

(f) Discuss and evaluate the effectiveness of legislation and
court decisions on prejudice and discrimination.

(g) Discuss the possible effect of revised laws in helping
people overcome stereotypes about other groups. Use
some of the research cited earlier in this book with your
students. Case studies make a fine group way to get at
and talk about key issues.

(h) Define responsibilities of all citizens regarding civil rights
laws and court decisions. Discuss moral as well as legal
considerations.

(i) Study the legislative recommendations of the United
States Civil Rights Commission. Investigate the kinds of
groups blocking recommended legislation.

(j) Trace the changing influence of nationality, religious,
racial, and socioeconomic groups in politics.

(k) Investigate the political structure of your own community or city, and see how it faces controversial issues,
what groups oppose facing them and acting upon them,
and discuss the civic and moral responsibilities of political leaders.

4. Problems of American Democracy and Contemporary Issues

(a) Review the kinds of issues alluded to in the article used
at the beginning of this section, "How U.S. 'Appears' to
One-Town World." In a newspaper or magazine, under-
line passages or phrases which describe current problems
in American life. For example, from several pages of a
widely read newspaper, these generalizations were
drawn, and articles from the newspaper were mounted
to substantiate the generalizations.

i. Americans want to help less fortunate people in

other countries, but Americans disagree about how this should be done.

   II. Americans want to help less fortunate people in their own country but disagree about how this should be done.

   III. Some Americans are determined to make progress on integration and provide equal opportunity for all.

   IV. Some Americans do not really believe that all people should have equal opportunities.

   V. Crime and juvenile delinquency are increasing in America.

   VI. Unemployment is increasing (or decreasing) in America.

   VII. Growing numbers of Americans are concerned about the problems connected with old age (health, education, recreation, etc.).

(b) Have students give true and false illustrations of what might be termed prejudice, ethnocentrism, stereotyping, and scapegoating.

(c) Study the effects of prejudice, segregation and discrimination on the following:

   I. Victims of discrimination or prejudice. Involve students in a discussion about how they felt when discriminated against or left out of a group for reasons other than ability. Role-play a situation in which a student is excluded from a student or neighborhood activity, with a member of the majority group playing the role of the victim.

   II. The discriminator or prejudiced person.

   III. U.S. international relations. Interview foreign students who will express frankly the reactions of their countrymen to news of discrimination in the United States.

(d) Help students find ways to investigate and assess the extent of prejudice and stereotyping.

   I. Discuss misconceptions about crime and race, and the proper and improper use of crime statistics.

   II. Assign a group of students to investigate several TV programs having to do with crime, and report on the extent of stereotyping.

   III. Evaluate the relationship of national origin, race and socioeconomic status to the social problems of mental illness, physical health, juvenile delinquency, crime, alcoholism, and drug addiction.

   IV. Analyze the relation of race and nationality to the "property values" of housing.

   V. Discuss whether there are any innate differences in intelligence between racial groups.

   VI. Give students tests, such as the Bogardus Social Distance Scale, to reveal their prejudices. Discuss those revealed, and the reasons why students think they have them.

(e) Discrimination and segregation

   I. Discuss the differences between prejudice and discrimination, and between nondiscrimination and integration.

   II. Study the past and present status of problems of discrimination and segregation based on race, religion, or national origin in the nation, state, and local community. Compare reports of President Truman's Committee on Civil Rights and the current United States Commission on Civil Rights. Debate the merits of literacy and educational qualifications to vote. Role-play a discriminatory voter registrar interviewing a Negro applying to vote. Study the record of the Peace Corps (Domestic) in helping southern Negroes register to vote during the summer of 1964.

III. Interview Negro veterans concerning their experiences with discrimination or segregation in the armed services. Study the way the various branches of the armed services were desegregated. Investigate attitudes of all groups before and after desegregation.

IV. Public schools and higher education: Analyze the patterns of racial composition at the elementary, secondary, and college levels of your local community. Examine the relationship of economic status and housing restrictions to school integration. Can you find evidence that community and school policy makers are cognizant of these kinds of segregation, and if so, what positive steps are they taking? Debate proposed solutions to the problem of *de facto* segregation in schools. Evaluate the history of religious, ethnic, racial, and geographical quota restrictions in college admission practices.

V. Employment: Interview local minority-group leaders as to their groups' experiences with discrimination in employment. Evaluate the causes of employment discrimination; e.g., fear of employee or customer reaction. Investigate union policies concerning employment. Interview local employers regarding policies toward hiring, especially nondiscriminatory hiring, the representation of minority persons in various job classifications in their employ, and their own personal feelings and ideas. Role-play an incident of job discrimination.

VI. Public and private housing: Discuss the relationship of segregation in housing to segregation in other aspects of community life. Examine the interrelationship of income and minority-group status to equalizing housing opportunity. Evaluate the common objections to integration in housing. Discuss alternative ways of responding to a racially changing neighborhood. Collect news items, pictures, and stories about responses to new neighbors by groups of different race or ethnic origins.

VII. Public accommodations: Interview minority-group classmates or adults to learn what situations they have encountered where they learned that they were not welcome, how they felt, and what happened when they tried to patronize a discriminatory establishment. Interview local proprietors of public accommodations (restaurants, motels, barber shops, bowling alleys, etc.) as to their policies and the reasons behind policies for serving and not serving.

VIII. Law enforcement: Study Negro newspaper charges of police brutality. Investigate the demonstrations in protest of alleged police brutality. Interview a police official regarding the problems of self-protection and law enforcement without infringing on civil rights. Find out whether Negroes are represented on your community's police force.

IX. Social discrimination: Study various extracurricular activities in your school and nearby schools. What is their membership pattern and what practices do they exercise in inviting participation by students of differing racial, religious, national origin, or socioeconomic groups.

X. Investigate the practice of self-segregation by minority groups in the area of housing, employment, and extracurricular school and informal associations. Discuss whether it is a problem, and if it is, what are some possible solutions.

XI. Appraise the effects of various organizations on human rights. Find out the avowed purposes of such organizations as Human Rights Councils, Urban League, Anti-Defamation League of B'nai B'rith, Human Relations Councils, NAACP, CORE, etc. Investigate the ways they attempt to implement these purposes.

(f) Investigate causes of discrimination, prejudice and stereotyping.

I. Write on such themes as "My Prejudices and How I Think I Got Them."

II. Survey the use of racial labels and stereotypes in newspaper stories of crime.

III. Evaluate the stereotyping of nationality and race in television and movie drama with respect to speech, names, physical characteristics and socioeconomic backgrounds.

IV. Also investigate cartoons, books, comic books, and newspaper comic strips.

(g) Investigate public and private agencies that combat prejudice and discrimination.

I. Visit their offices and facilities; invite their staff representatives to talk with the class and answer questions; participate, if possible, in a project sponsored by one of these agencies.

(h) Discuss and evaluate alternative solutions to the problems of discrimination and segregation, especially *de facto* segregation.

Legislation and court decisions	Quota systems
Economic boycotts	Censorship
Sit-in demonstrations and Freedom Rides	Formal education
	Propaganda
Domestic Peace Corps	Intergroup contact
Civil disobedience	Group retraining
Education	Attitude change

School redistricting

"Pairing" schools in differing sections

Bussing pupils to effect racial balance for equal educational opportunity

Education of adults in differing ethnic groups

(i) Study the process of rumor and hearsay and its effect on intergroup relations.

(j) Study propaganda techniques and ways to combat them.

(k) Analyze current interreligious conflicts.

5. Geography

Modern geography is concerned with both place (or location and environment) and man's interaction with his environment, both now and in the past. Study today must include consideration of man's growing ability to change his environment through modern transportation and communication, and through modern technological advances.

(a) Study the influence of climate, topography, and natural resources on such differences among ethnic groups, and between individuals of the same racial or religious groups as to

Skin color	Modes of communication
Other physical differences	Recreation
Food	Health
Clothing	Family life
Shelter	Isolation
Modes of transportation	Cultural achievements
Type of culture developed	Industrial achievements

(b) Examine the effects of cultural and geographic accessibility on racial-cultural similarity and achievement.

(c) Study the changes in natural resources in selected areas of our own country and the world. For instance, would a list of natural resources before the Civil War and now be the same or different?

(d) What has industrialization done to change types of crops grown, methods of mining and manufacturing, types of jobs that were directly related to geographic location and climate?

(e) What effects have geography had on education? On the development and course of wars? On economic development? On the development of the European Common Market? On the routing of international traffic and services?

6. World Cultures and World History

These courses essentially concern cultures other than our own but include our own as well. World Cultures courses concentrate on developing understanding of the major cultures of the world through examination of customs, folkways, religions, mores, geographic setting, political traditions, literature, music, art, and history as it pertains to these topics.

The real aim of a World Cultures course should be to help students understand that other cultures cannot be judged by our cultural standards. Through gaining more understanding of other cultures, their problems, and their aspirations, constant application can be made to intergroup educational implications in the United States.

World History is closely related inasmuch as history well taught seeks to help students understand the underlying causes of behavior by people in other times and places, as well as the events that represent the behavior of individuals and of societies.

World Cultures, World History, and World Literature, then, should be closely coordinated among English and social science teachers so that teachers and students can participate in depth experiences underlying intergroup education in all times and places. Cause and effect go hand in hand, but dates alone are soon forgotten because they lack substance and meaning for the student.

The study of races, religions, immigration, and contributions should provide the types of learning experiences already suggested in this chapter. Topics such as Hitler's treatment of the Jews relate directly to intergroup education. Teachers should do much more than gloss over the topic because it is an unpleasant subject. The treatment of the Jews by the Nazis does influence the lives of Jews, their attitude toward each other, and the attitude of others toward them all over the world. Russian pogroms and colonialism are related topics.

The struggle for independence from colonialism is as old as the world itself. Our own country fought the Revolutionary War to be rid of colonial control, and others around the world are daily fighting battles for this same reason.

Students might debate the meaning of "Readiness for Freedom." Does readiness for freedom occur while one is dominated? Does it automatically occur when one is free to run one's own affairs? How are decisions about government of newly independent nations made? Why is a large part of the world today Communist? What are the elements of Communism that appeal to underdeveloped nations?

What are the responsibilities of democracies to help underdeveloped nations? These questions and many others rightfully belong in curriculum that helps young people take their rightful place in the affairs of this country and of the world. Can any country today afford to live in the midst of plenty when others in the world are starving? What does the message at the base of the Statue of Liberty, gift of France, really mean to most Americans? What does the statue mean to the millions who have seen its guiding light as they approached the shores of the United States for the first time?

> Give me your tired, your poor,
> Your huddled masses yearning to breathe free
> The wretched refuse of your teeming shore.

> Send these, the homeless, tempest-tost to me,
> I lift my lamp beside the golden door.

C. *Modern foreign languages*

Courses in modern foreign languages offer excellent opportunities for considering the cultures in which the languages developed. Modern teaching utilizes the audio-lingual approach that encourages the use of tapes, films, and interchange of conversation.

Many media of communication and expression of the culture in which the language is spoken can contribute to rich understanding of the racial, religious, and ethnic cultures of the languages being studied. It is important to include the languages of Oriental, eastern European, Asian—including Russian—languages having different alphabets and intonations. Too often language instruction is confined to those that are of Latin derivation and classed as the Romance languages.

Language study is another way to point up the contributions of other world cultures to our own. Again, the activities appropriate to foreign language study should be coordinated with other departments such as English, art, music, homemaking, physical education, and social science departments.

D. *Science*

1. Study the effects of stereotyping on scientific perception and generalizations about people.
2. Study factors concerning group similarities and differences:
   (a) Anatomical and physiological differences and similarities between races, including blood composition.
   (b) The relation of environmental factors, diet, working conditions, and fatigue to race, physical health, and structure.
   (c) The variety of national, religious, racial, and socio-economic groups from which great scientists have come.

Study their biographies, their contributions, and the scientific advances that followed their initial work.

3. Investigate contributions of American Negroes to scientific advancement; for example, lesser known research figures such as Robert Rillieus, a Negro from New Orleans, who invented an evaporating pan that revolutionized the refining of raw sugar in the 1840's, and established the principles of industrial evaporation.

E. *Mathematics*

1. Assign individual students and groups of students to investigate origins of persons who contributed to the development of the science of mathematics.

2. Use data about various cultural groups or intergroup problems in applying statistical methods, making charts and graphs, and figuring trends. Information thus classified can include populations, occupations, and incomes.

3. Study different modes of measurement developed by different cultures; for instance, calendars, weights, money, and reasons for these differences.

4. Study the historic development of mathematical ideas and concepts through the contributions of such cultural groups as Chinese, Romans, Egyptians, Greeks, Hindus, and ancient Indian civilizations.

5. Investigate kinds of mathematical calculations needed and used in space exploration today. Among Russians and Americans, what are the ethnic origins of the originators of these calculations and ideas?

F. *Art*

Art forms involve attitudes, feelings, emotions, preferences, and personal tastes, for these determine to a large extent the manner in which we dress, furnish our living quarters, purchase items, and express ourselves. Art determines our reactions to the buildings, paintings, and sculpture we see. This is true for all people throughout the world. We can communicate with world neighbors of the present and past through the art they have created. To make or create something, man must have a design, and—no matter how crude the design—the designing is an art activity.

Art is a many-sided subject, and can be approached in many ways whether we are talking about education for the very young, older, or very old population. We can read about it, talk about it, see it, appreciate it, reproduce it, listen to it in music and in the spoken word. Art takes many forms, and teachers should be especially aware of all of the cultural media man has found in different times and different places and through which he has expressed himself, his hopes, his dreams, and his aspirations. We can learn much about what America really is through the contributions many Americans have made to the arts. The following activities cited for Music are just as appropriate for any of the arts.

G. *Music*

1. Define jazz; then trace its development. (This type of activity could be carried on with other types of music.)

   (a) A book such as Max Lerner's *America as a Civilization, Life, and Thought in the United States Today*[5] could be used for the following kinds of quotations and notes. Teachers would, of course, interpret and develop similar ideas with their students. Solicit student interpretations of the following quotations:

   "If you have to ask what jazz is, you'll never know."
   —Louis Armstrong

   "Man, if you don't know what it is, don't mess with it."—Fats Waller

[5] Max Lerner, *America as a Civilization, Life, and Thought in the United States Today* (New York, Simon and Schuster, 1957).

Lerner comments:

The more important musical idiom of America was the "ragtime" and "hot jazz" of the twenties, the "swing" of the thirties, the "cool jazz" of the forties, and "rock'n roll" of the fifties. These terms imply complex beat and rhythm, improvisation, and musicianly teamwork. . . .

The musicians took almost any tune, and what came out of the instruments was a miracle of transmutation—a delicate lacework of magic that intoxicated the senses and was especially tantalizing because it depended entirely upon the improvising of the moment and the inter-weaving of instruments caught in a common excitement. Since good jazz is evanescent, it must be captured and treasured in the memory. . . .

What remains primitive in it is the generic human impulses breaking through the strata of Western machine living which have threatened to overlay the instinctual life. . . .

The traditional elite music tends to make passive listeners out of its audiences. It is the music of the popular culture, with its widespread singing, dancing, and improvising jam sessions, that turns audiences into participants, bringing them closer to a dynamic and communal activity. This was also true of traditional music in its origins.

> (b) Investigate when and where jazz originated (no one knows this); New Orleans as "the cradle of jazz"; the quadrille (a French dance) containing some of the themes used in early jazz; jazz as played in the late 1800's by Negro American brass bands in street parades and funeral processions; instruments used in early brass bands, etc.
>
> (c) Transition periods and musicians connected with history of transition:
>
> | | |
> |---|---|
> | ragtime | swing |
> | blues | boogie-woogie |
> | Dixieland | bop |
> | Chicago | cool jazz |
>
> (d) Investigate the formal recognition of jazz from the first

New York stage presentation in 1905 through the "cool jazz" of the sixties.

(e) Report on some of the famous jazz bands, instrumentalists, or vocalists. Collect and listen to their recordings.

Bands and band leaders	Vocalists
Louis Armstrong and Hot Five	Bessie Smith
King Oliver's Creole Jazz	Ella Fitzgerald
Freddie Keppard	Mildred Bailey
Fate Marable	Anita O'Day
Bunk Johnson	Sophie Tucker
Kid Bolden's Band	Ethel Waters

Instrumentalists

Bix Beiderbecke—cornet
Louis Armstrong—trumpet
Muggsy Spanier—cornet
Jack Teagarden—trombone
Sidney Bechet—saxophone
Johnny Dodds—clarinet
Bunny Berigan—trumpet

2. Apply the same techniques to other kinds of music including:
   (a) Folk, including ballad and minstrel
   (b) Classical, including opera, operetta, symphony
   (c) Semiclassical
   (d) Musical comedy
   (e) War songs
   (f) Martial music
   (g) Religious music

3. The History, English, Music, Art, Dramatic Art, and Dance Departments could cooperate on any of the preceding or the following:

Playwriting	Concert soloists	Architecture
Acting	Choreography	Cartoons
Direction	Ballet	Commercial art

Scenic design	Modern dance	Sculpture
Movies	Popular dance	Ceramics
Television	Painting	Prose and poetry

At each stage, and through each department, emphasis should be on the contributions of *many* differing Americans to the culture of America and to the culture of the world. Young people must learn to understand that we live in an age of contrasts—of changing manners, cultures, philosophies, and morals. Knowledge can put man into space, but it can also make him feel more at home with his neighbors and his fellow citizens. Today's world requires today's knowledge and combines both enduring and changing values. Today's teachers will teach intergroup education deliberately and effectively so that provincialism does not cripple this or future generations.

Intergroup Education Opportunities Through School-Community Life and Group Life in School

Extracurricular and informal out-of-class activities are of significant importance to intergroup education. In these portions of school and community life, which are more subject to student control, the behavioral results of classroom education can be seen quite clearly. At the same time, student activities both during and after the regular school day offer unique opportunities for young people to practice the social skills of group participation and leadership that are essential to the achievement of democratic interpersonal relationships.

In Chapter 3, the nature of prejudice and stereotyping was discussed and the importance of interpersonal association across group lines as a critical deterrent to intergroup prejudices was substantiated. In the context of segregation, especially, economic, racial, social and religious differences exist in most areas of community life. Schools and communities can make no more valuable contributions than to assure opportunities for young people of different backgrounds to associate in common interests and projects. Where great diversity or homogeneity has existed, it is especially important that group activities should be *inclusive*, not *exclusive*.

One of the social skills for democratic living mentioned earlier was the ability to participate democratically and effectively in groups. In this there is no substitute for actual practice. Extracurricular clubs create opportunities for young people to practice techniques important to successful interpersonal relations. Learning to function in roles of leadership as well as group membership are vital components of intergroup skills. Leadership posts, therefore, should not be used simply as rewards for those who have already mastered academic and social skills, but should be used to provide as many students as possible with training and experience in developing group leadership.

For those students whose needs are not being met during the regular academic day through classroom grades and academic achievement, extracurricular activities may offer the only major area of school life where the underachiever or minority group student gains acceptance. School records can be seriously impaired, dropouts become more numerous, and behavior problems develop when students fail to acquire a feeling of *belonging*—of being needed and valued.

In studies done at the University of Chicago Center for Intergroup Education from 1952 to 1955, the extracurricular programs of seven different schools in various parts of the country were studied. It was concluded that ". . . the lack of a sense of belonging (in school extracurricular life) affects self-expectations and motivation regarding academic success; and therefore, also academic achievement, because integration of individuals in school groups seems to enhance motivation for learning, while distintegration, cleavage, and isolation lessen effort and motivation."[6]

Probably the most important starting place to ensure that student

[6] Hilda Taba, *School Culture, Studies of Participation and Leadership*, Washington, D.C., American Council on Education, 1955, pp. 114–115.

intergroup activities make a maximum contribution to the intergroup education of a school is to study patterns of leadership, participation, and associations in the student group life of school, both during the regular school day, and after school hours. This type of evaluation would be appropriate for any school intergroup education committee, and could include those teachers involved with various clubs, sports, musical and dramatic organizations. The "Participation Schedule"[7] is a frequently used device for analyzing school group life. It consists of questionnaires to be answered by students, club leaders, and sponsors, and is designed to indicate who is and who is not participating in extracurricular activities, its leadership positions, and the reasons for these patterns.

Another dimension of student group life worthy of close study is the pattern of association among students during the informal activities of the school day. These occur in the corridors between classes, on playgrounds during recess periods, during the lunch hour, at school assemblies, and at plays, concerts, and athletic events. This type of self-survey would attempt to answer the following questions:

1. Do the students of any group appear to segregate themselves and avoid association with other students?
2. How friendly and cooperative, as opposed to tolerant, are the relations among students of different groups?
3. Are students elected to office without either favorable or unfavorable regard for their group membership?
4. Are leadership positions in clubs and activities shared by students of all racial and ethnic groups?
5. What specific steps are being taken by each club or activity to make all students feel welcome to active membership and maximum participation?

[7] Detailed instructions for administering Participation Schedules are given in Hilda Taba, Elizabeth H. Brady, John T. Robinson and William E. Vickery, *Diagnosing Human Relations Needs*, Washington, D.C., American Council on Education, 1951, pp. 48–70, 149–153.

6. Are scholarship or social ability requirements for student organizations so high that they may eliminate participation by those who most need the experience?

7. Are the financial or dress requirements for some of the groups such that many from lower socioeconomic groups would be excluded?

8. Does religion, race, nationality, or socioeconomic status seem to be a factor in the membership practices of any groups?

9. Are students of particular groups applying in disproportionate numbers for participation in certain activities and not for others?

10. Is the racial, religious, national, and socioeconomic ratio of the school also represented in about the same proportion in most of the activities?

11. Do the schedules, sponsorship, and types of activities meet up-to-date needs (social and interest) of all groups of students?

12. Are some of the clubs *service-type clubs* with activities such as community volunteer work, social action, conservation and beautification, orienting new students to school and community, school assembly exchange, student employment, etc.?

Fundamental changes in student activities programs are complex undertakings, requiring the combined efforts of school staffs. Though complex and time-consuming, the basic importance of this aspect of school life warrants serious attention inasmuch as it probably has inestimable effect on student intergroup attitudes and behavior.

The Community-School Program

A number of communities, particularly urban and suburban centers, are developing programs that continue long after the regular school day, and encompass groups ranging in age from the cradle to the rocking chair. In New Haven, Connecticut, for instance, valuable dimensions have been added to education, and to the utilization of school buildings and facilities, through community-school programs such as

1. Pre-kindergarten classes for culturally deprived youngsters who are not able to function according to the school's expectations when they enter school at the regular age.
2. After-school talent and enrichment clubs.
3. Volunteer tutoring programs and open library study centers.
4. Higher Horizon Programs, both during and after the school day.
5. Helping-teacher assistance programs for inner-city schools.
6. Summer school centers.
7. Public school-college assistance programs.
8. Junior and senior high school work-study programs.
9. Prevocational and pretechnical programs.
10. Community-school projects, and others.

These programs are made possible through an organization known as Community Progress, Incorporated. Together with a physical renewal program for lifting the face of the city during the past decade, Mayor Richard C. Lee envisioned accompanying and necessary *human renewal;* thus Community Progress, Inc., became the instrument through which many organizations funneled and received funds, and drew upon wide talents for guidance, participation, and administration. Presently, under the directorship of a former president of the Board of Education who gained valuable insight into educational needs and fiscal limitations to meet those needs, the organization distributes local, state, and federal funds to Pilot Projects and other community enterprises. As programs prove effective and advisable, it is intended that municipal budgetary groups will incorporate them into their permanent programs. Without initial catalytic impetus and financial support, many of these projects would still be "on paper."

Patterns are evolving whereby schools become centers for year-round, and clock-round activities. Teachers, community agencies, area colleges and universities, and neighborhood associations together with citizens of all ages are making constant use of modern school facilities. Classrooms hum from dawn to dusk and long after; school-community libraries are centers of activity, as are auditoriums, teen-age lounges, and senior centers. Summertime finds a wide variety of intellectual, recreational, and cultural pursuits by children and adults of all ages. Evenings find people of all cultural, ethnic, racial, religious, and socioeconomic groups pursuing courses of study ranging from Adult Literacy to Zoology.

Inside and outside of a center like the Conte Community School, one would have difficulty realizing that this was the decaying heart of a slum area just a few years ago. Around it, the brownstone town houses of another era are taking on new façades and new characters as intercultural and interracial families are attracted to improved living conditions in the heart of a city. Daily we see that widely divergent ages, cultures, religions, and races can function side by side to enrich and benefit each other's lives.

Unfortunately, too few parts of our country have been willing or interested in putting forth this kind of community effort, for daily, too, we see and hear and read about old hatreds, old stereotypes, and old prejudices popping up to defeat real intergroup education and to poison the minds of another generation. The models are too few and community-school action too negligible.

Community and school leaders would do well to visit and study those models that do exist, and ask themselves how aspects of these models could be adapted to improve civic pride and educational experiences for the human and physical renewals vital to all segments of our population.

Looking Ahead

The war on prejudice, on lack of educational opportunities, and on socioeconomic deprivation should never end. Every college professor, every community and civic leader, every member of every board of education or other community policy-making group, every school administrator, every teacher, and every student should be involved in the task force that fights ignorance.

Every citizen needs to act with knowledge, good judgment, and resourcefulness toward the goal of educating today's children and youth so that they may be fully functioning, self-educating citizens of the future.

Intergroup education is dependent upon knowledgeable innovation—societal *and* curricular. Today's citizens need to be particularly cognizant of changing social and cultural demands that require

New and different emphases in the education of children and youth.

Different emphases in the concept of the *public* school.

Emphases on the qualities essential in teaching.

Imaginative ways to support, strengthen, and extend actions that will develop our most valuable national resource—our children and youth.

Community leaders and educators who are increasingly able to identify issues and contribute to their solutions, initiating change when appropriate.

It becomes an urgent responsibility to help every young person move from thinking that life is his own personal *privilege or prison* to recognizing that it is everyone's privilege or prison, depending upon collective intergroup action.

Although the problems of modern living are complex, and forces that control them are vague, we cannot doubt our ability to deal with them. The stakes are too great, and individuals must exert power over their own destinies; education is the catalyst that can be placed in the hands of people to give them the power to *control* change—not merely adapt to it. America's schools can still become the link so long missing in raising the productive capacity, dignity, and worth of all citizens.

Our schools and communities today are grappling with the problems of the young adult, the dropout, the unemployed, the aged, the family, the disadvantaged, and the apathetic citizen. It is not the job of the school alone to help society develop constructive attitudes, recognize and assume their citizenship responsibilities, learn how to live together as neighbors, and assume responsibility for personal and community growth and change. It is a cooperative job in which schools can give unprecedented leadership with the sanction of an awakened public. Without cooperative action, the Bill of Rights, the Bill of Human Rights, and our Constitution itself become meaningless bits of paper to be memorized and then forgotten. This was never the intention of their originators.

It is time we place a premium on the "openness" that will help bridge the gap between indifference and caring—between theory and practice—between lip service and action—between research and implementation—between public schools and colleges of teacher education—and between community policy-makers and educators. Whatever we dare to dream, think, plan, and undertake, let us remember that it is not for the glory of one office or institution. It is for children—for future citizenship—for dynamic action that will continue on in the world we leave. What kind of a world will it be? Do we care enough to change it?

CHAPTER **6**

INTERGROUP EDUCATION SOURCES
AND RESOURCES

SOME OF THESE BOOKS and materials have been referred to in preceding chapters. Others are recommended for specific groups and purposes. These lists are not intended to be exhaustive or final; they are, however, representative. They are designed to serve as guides for study groups, whether these be community groups, community-school groups, or school groups. The resources are arranged as follows:

Books, Periodicals, and Pamphlets for Adults and Older Students
    —Books (see also "The Negro in America")
    —Pamphlets, Periodicals, and Articles
Intergroup Education Films and Filmstrips
    —For All Ages
    —For Elementary School Children
    —For Junior High School Students
    —For Senior High School Students and Adults
Books for Primary and Middle School Children
More Books and Pamphlets for Older Students
The Negro in America—Annotated Bibliography
Records for All Ages
Teaching Units and Bibliographies
Source Information

BOOKS, PERIODICALS, AND PAMPHLETS FOR
ADULTS AND OLDER STUDENTS

BOOKS

Alpenfels, Ethel J., *Sense and Nonsense About Race,* New York, Friendship Press, 1957. An anthropologist discusses the myths about race, giving facts that are convincingly and impressively presented. Included are the accepted scientific repudiations of eight typical beliefs.

Ashton-Warner, Sylvia, *The Teacher,* New York, Simon and Schuster, Inc., 1963. Sensitive writing, and magnificent portrayal of teaching children who are actually "different." You won't be able to put it down until you complete it.

Bendix, Reinhard, and Lipset, Seymour M., *Class, Status, and Power,* New York, Free Press of Glencoe, Inc., 1953.

Braithwaite, Edward R., *To Sir with Love,* Englewood Cliffs, Prentice-Hall, Inc., 1962. An unforgettable, inspiring chronicle of the courage and patience of a teacher who was a stranger and of a different race. A true story of the birth of understanding in a teen-age classroom.

Brown, Spencer, *They See for Themselves, a Documentary Approach to Intercultural Education in the High School,* New York, Harper and Brothers, 1954.

Cantril, T., *Tensions That Cause Wars,* Urbana, University of Illinois Press, 1950.

Chandler, B. J., Stiles, Lindley J., and Kitsuse, John I., *Education in Urban Society,* New York, Dodd, Mead & Company, 1963.

Clayton, Ed, *Martin Luther King: The Peaceful Warrior,* Englewood Cliffs, Prentice-Hall, Inc., 1964.

Cole, Steward G., and Vickery, William E., *Intercultural Education*

165

in American Schools; Proposed Objectives and Methods, New York, Harper and Brothers, 1943.

Conant, James Bryant, *Slums and Suburbs,* New York, McGraw-Hill Book Company, Inc., 1961.

Cook, Lloyd and Elaine, *School Problems in Human Relations,* New York, McGraw-Hill Book Company, Inc., 1957.

Davis, Allison, *Social Class Influence Upon Learning,* Cambridge, Harvard University Press, 1948.

Dean, John P., and Rosen, Alex A., *A Manual of Intergroup Relations,* Chicago, University of Chicago Press, 1955.

Department of Supervisors and Directors of Instruction of the National Education Association, National Council of Teachers of English and Society for Curriculum Study, *American All, Studies in Intercultural Education,* National Education Association, Washington, D.C., 1942.

Dollard, John, *Caste and Class in a Southern Town,* Garden City, Anchor Books, Doubleday, 1957.

Douglas, William O., *Mr. Lincoln and the Negroes; The Long Road to Equality,* New York, Atheneum Publishers, 1963. Supreme Court Justice Douglas handles the details of Lincoln's conscience and actions like the accomplished jurist he is, and analyzes some of the pressures on a President.

DuBois, Rachel D., *Build Together Americans,* New York, Hinds, Hayden & Eldredge, 1945.

Duncan, Ethel M., *Democracy's Children, Adventures in Intercultural Understanding for the Elementary School,* New York, Hinds, Hayden and Eldredge, 1945.

Eells, Kenneth, et al., *Intelligence and Cultural Differences,* Chicago, University of Chicago Press, 1951.

Epstein, B. R., and Forster, A., *Some of My Best Friends,* New York, Farrar, Straus, Cudahy, Inc., 1962.

Franklin, John Hope, *The Emancipation Proclamation,* Garden City, Doubleday & Co., Inc., 1963. In this book Professor Franklin, a well-known historian, has put Lincoln's document into historical perspective.

Giles, Harry, *The Integrated Classroom,* New York, Basic Books, Inc., 1959.

Goodman, Mary E., *Race Awareness in Young Children,* Reading, Mass., Addison-Wesley Publishing Co., Inc., 1952.

Graham, Shirley, *There Was Once a Slave,* New York, Julian Messner Inc., 1947. This volume can be highly recommended because of the literary qualities of this account of the life of Frederick Douglas, and because the author received the publisher's award for the "Best Book Combating Intolerance in America."

Hartmann, Edward G., *The Movement to Americanize the Immigrant,* New York, Columbia University Press, 1948.

Heaton, Margaret M., and Lewis, Helen B., *Reading Ladders for Human Relations, Revised and Enlarged Edition,* Washington, American Council on Education, 1955.

Hentoff, Nat, *The New Equality,* New York, Viking Press, Inc., 1964. A very recent book by an author who is close to the civil rights revolution through his experiences as a jazz specialist and writer. He explores the contradictions of middle class attitudes attributed to teachers, among others.

Hill, Herbert, *Soon One Morning,* New York, Alfred A. Knopf, Inc., 1963. Also a relatively new book exploring new writing by American Negroes between 1940 and 1962. There is variety, depth, and brilliance in these selections from more than two dozen contemporary literary artists.

Hollingshead, A. B. and Redlich, R., *Social Class and Mental Illness,* New York, John Wiley & Sons, Inc., 1958.

Hunt, J. McV., *Intelligence and Experience,* New York, Ronald Press Co., 1961.

Inge, William Ralph, *Labels and Libels,* New York, Harper and Brothers, 1929.

James, Leonard F., *The Supreme Court in American Life,* Chicago, Scott, Foresman and Company, 1964.

Kilpatrick, William H., and Van Til, William, *Intercultural Attitudes in the Making,* New York, Harper and Brothers, 1947.

LaFarge, John S. J., *No Postponement,* Longmans, Green & Company, 1950.

Lippmann, Walter, *Public Opinion,* Baltimore, Penguin Books, Inc., 1946.

Lowenthal, L., and Guterman, N., *Prophets of Deceit,* New York, Harper and Brothers, 1949.

Mandelbaum, Seymour J., *The Social Setting of Intolerance,* Chicago, Scott, Foresman, 1964. Contents are indicated by subtitle, "The Know Nothings, The Red Scare, and McCarthyism."

Marrow, A. J., *Changing Patterns of Prejudice,* New York, Clifton Company, 1962.

Miller, Arthur, *Focus,* New York, Reynal & Hitchcock, 1945.

Murphy, G., *In the Minds of Men,* New York, Basic Books, Inc., 1963.

Noar, Gertrude, *The Junior High School—Today and Tomorrow,* New York, Prentice-Hall, Inc., 1961.

Noar, Gertrude, *Teaching and Learning the Democratic Way,* New York, Prentice-Hall, Inc., 1962.

Passow, A. Harry, *Education in Depressed Areas,* Bureau of Publications, Teachers College, New York, Columbia University Press, 1963.

Pettigrew, T. F., and Campbell, E. Q., *Christians in Racial Crisis*, Washington, Public Affairs Press, 1959.

Pettigrew, Thomas, *Profile of the Negro American*, New York, D. Van Nostrand Company, 1964.

Redden, John D., and Ryan, Rances A., *Intercultural Education*, Milwaukee, The Bruce Publishing Company, 1951.

Reissman, Frank, *The Culturally Deprived Child*, Harper and Row, 1962.

Rose, Arnold M., *Race, Prejudice and Discrimination; Readings in Intergroup Education in the United States*, New York, Alfred A. Knopf, Inc., 1951.

Rose, Peter II, *They And We*, New York, Random House, Inc., 1964.

Roy, R. L., *Apostles of Discord*, Boston, Beacon Press, 1953.

Saenger, Gerhart, *The Social Psychology of Prejudice*, New York, Harper and Brothers, 1953.

Sears, Robert D., et al., *Patterns of Child Rearing*, Row, Peterson & Company, 1957.

Sexton, Patricia, *Education and Income*, New York, Viking Press, Inc., 1961.

Simpson, G. W., and Yonger, J. M., *Racial and Cultural Minorities*, New York, Harper and Brothers, 1958.

Solomon, Barbara M., *Ancestors and Immigrants*, Cambridge, Harvard University Press, 1956.

Starkey, Marion L., *The Devil in Massachusetts*, New York, Alfred A. Knopf, Inc., 1950.

Stendler, Celia B., and Martin, William E., *Intergroup Education in Kindergarten-Primary Grades*, New York, The Macmillan Company, 1953.

Summers, M., *The History of Witchcraft*, New Hyde Park, N.Y., University Books, 1956.

Taba, Hilda, *School Culture; Studies of Participation and Leadership*,* 1955.

Taba, Hilda, *With Perspective on Human Relations; A Study of Group Dynamics in an Eighth Grade*,* 1955.

Taba, Hilda, Brady, Elizabeth H., and Robinson, John T. *Intergroup Education in Public Schools*, 1952. Washington, D.C., American Council on Education.

Tead, Diana, *What Is Race?*, UNESCO, 1952.

Trager, Helen G., and Yarrow, Marion R., *They Learn What They*

* These and other books by Dr. Taba are published by the American Council on Education, Washington, D.C.

Live, Prejudice in Young Children, New York, Harper and Brothers, 1952.

U.S. Department of Health, Education and Welfare, Office of Education, *Improving English Skills of Culturally Different Youth in Large Cities,* and *School-Home Partnership in Depressed Urban Neighborhoods,* U.S. Government Printing Office, 1964.

Van Til, William, *The Making of a Modern Educator,* Indianapolis, The Bobbs-Merrill Company, 1961.

Warner, W. Lloyd, *Yankee City,* New Haven, Yale University Press, 1963.

Whyte, William F. Jr., *Street Corner Society,* Chicago, University of Chicago Press, 1955.

Young, Whitney W., *To Be Equal,* New York, McGraw-Hill Book Company, Inc.

PAMPHLETS AND PERIODICALS

"Addendum: A Five-Year Report on Desegregation in Washington, D.C. Schools." Report by Carl F. Hansen, Anti-Defamation League (ADL), 1960. This addendum is the author's follow-up report to his earlier report, "Miracle of Adjustment: Desegregation in Washington, D.C." Also published by ADL.

Administrative Committee on Intercultural Education, "Promising Practices in Intergroup Education," Detroit Board of Education, 1947.

Allport, Gordon W., "ABC's of Scapegoating," ADL, 1963, 44 pp.

Allport, Gordon W., "The Resolution of Intergroup Tensions," National Conference of Christians and Jews.

American Association of School Administrators, "From Sea to Shining Sea—Administrators Handbook for Intergroup Education," NEA, 1947, 64 pp.

Anti-Defamation League of B'Nai B'Rith, "Behind the Headlines," "Regional Problems and Issues in Human Relations Education," "How Do You Talk About People?," and many others. See their catalogue and other references here.

Association for Supervision and Curriculum Development (ASCD), *Cultural Understanding in a World Community,* Volume 19, No. 8, May 1962; *Continuity of Teacher Education,* 1964, 1965, and 1966; as well as Yearbooks, which are among the finest definitions of educational concerns during the past decades, and monthly issues of *Educational Leadership,* Journal of the ASCD, Washington, D.C.

Bard, Harry, "Teachers and the Community, An In-Service Program in Action," National Conference of Christians and Jews.

Beauchamp, Mary; Llewellyn, Ardelle; and Worley, Vivienne S., "Building Brotherhood: What Can Elementary Schools Do?" National Conference of Christians and Jews.

Benne, Bradford, and Lippitt, "Group Dynamics and Social Action," ADL.

Benne, Kenneth D., "The Strategic Situation in Intergroup Education U.S.A.: 1960." Paper presented at Intergroup Education Conference, Institute of Human Relations, January 18, 1960, American Jewish Committee (mimeographed).

Bogue, Donald J. and Seim, Emerson, "Components of Population Change in Suburban and Central City Populations of Standard Metropolitan Areas," *Rural Sociology,* Sept.–Dec., 1956.

Bostwick, Prudence, "Brotherhood: What Can Secondary Schools Do?" National Conference of Christians and Jews.

Clark, Kenneth B., "How to Protect Children Against Prejudice," Child Study, 1951.

Committee of Religion and Education of the American Council on Education, "The Function of the Public Schools in Dealing with Religion," 1953.

Corsi, Edward, "Paths to the New World," ADL.

Davidson, Helen and Lang, Gerhard, "Children's Perceptions of Their Teacher's Feelings Toward Them Related to Self-Perception, School Achievement, and Behavior," *Journal of Experimental Education,* 1960.

Detroit Board of Education, "The Human Touch, A Guide in Human Relations," published by Detroit Board of Education, 1959.

Division Against Discrimination, "Know Your Human Relations, A Digest of Information," New Jersey Department of Education, Trenton, 1956.

Division on Civil Rights, "Civil Rights in New Jersey; A Resource Unit," New Jersey Department of Education, 1960. (Also contact your own State Education Department and your state's Human Relations Commission, Civil Rights Commission, or Equal Opportunities Commission.)

Dodson, Dan W., "The Changing Neighborhood," *Educational Leadership,* ASCD, May, 1961, 18:497–501.

Drudling, Aleda, "Stirrings in Big Cities; Philadelphia," *NEA Journal,* February, 1962, 51:48–51.

Epstein, Charlotte, "Evaluating Intergroup Relations Education," reprinted from the *Bulletin of the National Association of Secondary School Principals,* October, 1960, American Jewish Committee.

Ebony. The *Life* magazine of the Negro press should be familiar to adults as well as to middle-school children, and older students.

Educational Policies Commission, NEA, "Education and the Disadvantaged American," 1962.

Freedomways. A quarterly review with literary appeal based on the Negro freedom movement. Current literature and issues in each publication.

Goodman, Mary E., "A Primer for Parents," ADL #G352.

Grambs, Jean D., "Group Processes in Intergroup Education," National Conference of Christians and Jews.

Grambs, Jean D., "Understanding Intergroup Relations," NEA, 1960

Gray, J. S. and Thompson, A. H., "The Ethnic Prejudices of Negro and White College Students," *Journal of Abnormal and Social Psychology,* 1953, 48:311–313.

Handlin, Oscar and Mary, "Danger in Discord," ADL.

Hartford Board of Education, "Education in the Changing Urban Community," Hartford, Conn., Board of Education, 1963 (mimeographed).

Harmon Foundation. This organization's specialty is information on Negro arts and artists, and they will make arrangements to lend paintings.

Heaton, Margaret M., "Feelings Are Facts," Nat'l Conference of Christians and Jews, 1951.

Hill, Wilhelmina, and Mackintosh, Helen K., "How Children Learn About Human Rights," U.S. Department of Health, Education, and Welfare, 1951.

Horowitz, Eugene L., "Development of Attitudes Toward Negroes," *Archives of Psychology,* 1936, No. 194.

Human Relations Committee, "Handbook on Human Relations," Department of Instruction, Cincinnati Public Schools, 1959.

Kilpatrick, William H., "Modern Education and Better Human Relations," ADL.

Lane, Howard A., "Shall Children Too Be Free?" ADL.

Lee, Irving J., "How Do You Talk About People?" ADL.

Lee, Ralph, "Stirrings in Big Cities: Detroit," *NEA Journal,* March, 1962.

Morrison, J. Cayce, "The Puerto Rican Study, 1953–1957: A Report on the Education and Adjustment of Puerto Rican Pupils in the Public Schools of the City of New York," New York City Board of Education, 1958.

NAACP (National Association for the Advancement of Colored People), "Negro Heroes of Emancipation," 1964.

NCRAC (National Community Relations Advisory Council), "De Facto Segregation in Public Schools," a position paper for the guidance of community agencies, particularly Jewish communities and agencies, 1964.

New Haven Board of Education, "Proposals for Promoting Equality of Educational Opportunity and Dealing with the Problems of Racial Imbalance in Schools," June, 1964, New Haven Board of Education, New Haven, Conn.

New York Public Library, "Books About Negro Life for Children and Adults," Annotated.

Overstreet, Bonaro W., "The Responsibility Is Ours," ADL.

Pennsylvania Department of Public Instruction, "Pennsylvania Teaches for Better World Relations and Intercultural Understanding," and "Our Greatest Challenge—Human Relations," DPI, Harrisburg, Pa., 1955–62.

Philadelphia Board of Education, "The Development of Intergroup Education in the Philadelphia Public Schools," 1960 (mimeographed).

Raab, Earl, and Lipset, Seymour M., "Prejudice and Society," ADL.

Radke, Marion, "Children's Attitudes Toward Minority Groups," unpublished summary summarized in R. Lippitt and M. Radke, "New Trends in the Investigation of Prejudice," *The Annals of the American Academy of Political and Social Science,* March, 1964.

Rose, Arnold, "The Roots of Prejudice," UNESCO, 1951.

Silberman, Charles E., "The City and the Negro," *Fortune* magazine, March, 1962.

U.S. Department of Labor, "The Economic Situation of Negroes in the United States," Washington, D.C., 1962.

Valien, Bonita, "The St. Louis Story," ADL, 1956.

Wright, Betty Atwell, "Do You Think They Hurt Our Friends?" *Grade Teacher,* Feb., 1962.

Wright, Betty Atwell, "When Parents Teach Too," *Childhood Education,* Feb., 1961.

"What High School Students Say: A Survey of Attitudes and Knowledge," ADL, 1961.

INTERGROUP EDUCATION FILMS AND FILMSTRIPS

Films and filmstrips have been listed according to their suitability for particular groups. These should be previewed for purpose intended and for the most effective use, inasmuch as some films listed in certain sections are equally suitable for other themes. Some films may be used for many age levels even though they are recommended for specific groups. These materials are arranged alphabetically within the following categories:

Anti-Semitism
Cities Today
Discrimination and Segregation
Fair Employment Practices
Fair Housing Practices
Immigrants, Newcomers, and Immigration
Intergroup Education in Schools
International Human Rights
Interreligious Understanding
Negro-Americans
Other Minority Groups
Prejudices and Stereotypes
Projects for Brotherhood
Racial Differences
World Friends

Loan, rental, or purchase sources are given, as well as the title, content-summary, and length, whenever possible. Check Source Information at the end of this chapter for full names and addresses of organizations distributing them.

Unless otherwise noted, materials are black and white; films are 16mm, and filmstrips are 35mm.

For All Ages

FILMS

IMMIGRANTS, NEWCOMERS, AND IMMIGRATION:

The Greenie

A story concerning a small Polish refugee boy, recently arrived in America. At first he is ridiculed and rejected by the youngsters in his block, but he is finally accepted by them as a fellow American. 10 minutes. Source: National Council of Christians and Jews.

Our People

This story of the contributions of various groups of Americans of many ethnic and racial heritages is narrated by Vincent Price.

The main theme is the diversity of people, and the principle of
equal opportunity. Color. 12 minutes. Source: Anti-Defamation
League.

Who Are the People of America?

Coronet magazine's documentary of the ways American freedoms
and customs are collective results of the contributions of many
immigrant groups—working and struggling together. Color. 10
minutes. Source: Coronet.

INTERRELIGIOUS UNDERSTANDING:

One God

Based on the book of the same name by Florence Mary Fitch,
this film features choral music of each faith—Protestant, Catholic, and Jewish—and has beautiful photography. 37 minutes.
Source: Anti-Defamation League.

Your Neighbor Celebrates

A high school group hears a rabbi describe the major Jewish
holidays: Rosh Hoshanah, Yom Kippur, Succoth, Passover, and
Shevuoth. The ceremonies are pictured through music and song.
26 minutes. Source: National Conference of Christians and Jews.

PREJUDICES AND STEREOTYPES:

Sing a Song of Friendship

Fine choral group singing of Irving Caesar's musical ballads with
messages of interracial, interreligious, and international harmony.
Illustrated with cartoons, and suitable for community singing.
Color. 20 minutes. Source: Anti-Defamation League, Jewish
Community Relations Council, and National Council of Chris-
tians and Jews.

RACIAL DIFFERENCES:

Brotherhood of Man

Based on the scientific pamphlet, "Races of Mankind," this animated cartoon presents the scientific facts concerning people
of all races, religions, and nationalities and how they are similar;
differences are presented as being superficial and due to accident

and environment. Color. 11 minutes. Source: Jewish Labor Committee.

FILMSTRIPS

NEGRO-AMERICANS:

George Washington Carver Story

The story of how Carver, nicknamed "the plant doctor," rendered invaluable service to his country, in spite of slavery and discrimination, by discovering many uses for the peanut. 72 frames. Source: Anti-Defamation League.

Outstanding Americans of Negro Origin

Full-color portraits and thumbnail sketches of 36 famous and outstanding Negro-Americans. With script. 56 frames. Sale only: $6.00. Harmon Foundation, Inc.

PREJUDICE AND STEREOTYPES:

About People

Based on the juvenile best seller *All About Us*, by Eva Knox Evans, this filmstrip shows why people live, play, work, and worship in different ways, but have essentially the same desires and needs. Discussion guide. Color. 63 frames. Source: Jewish Community Relations Council.

American Counterpoint

Demonstrates how people of various religions, racial and national origins, and differing culture groups have built and enriched this country. With script. Source: Philadelphia Fellowship Commission.

Little Songs on Big Subjects

This filmstrip has won eight national citations and its script has been broadcast over 2000 radio stations. It is Tin Pan Alley's contribution to American democracy and neighborliness—ideal for group singing. With recording, lyric sheets, and songbook. 68 frames. Source: Philadelphia Fellowship Commission.

RACIAL DIFFERENCES:

We Are All Brothers

Cartoon treatment used to present scientific facts concerning beliefs about racial differences. Based on Ruth Benedict's famous pamphlet, "The Races of Mankind." With 20-minute recording or script, or both. 56 frames. Source: Jewish Labor Committee.

For Elementary School Children

FILMS

HUMAN RIGHTS:

Heritage

An animated cartoon, in color, concerns human rights, moral values, and relationships between rights and responsibilities. 10 minutes. Source: Anti-Defamation League.

IMMIGRANTS, NEWCOMERS, AND IMMIGRATION:

The Princess In The Tower

A newcomer to a typical neighborhood feels lonely and rejected until she learns that acceptance means being a good neighbor, and accepting others as persons of equal worth each in his own way. Older elementary school-age children. 22 minutes. Source: Jewish Community Relations Council.

One People

Vincent Price relates the dramatic story of the settling of America. Animated cartoon. Color. Source: Anti-Defamation League.

Propaganda Techniques

Explains propaganda and its detection. This one can also be used in junior high school. Explains techniques and gives examples. 10 minutes. Source: Coronet Films.

Skipper Learns a Lesson

A delightful and humorous story of a little dog who learns that it is what people are on the inside, not their outside appearance, that counts. Color. 10 minutes. Source: Philadelphia Fellowship Commission, and Anti-Defamation League.

The Toymaker

This is a highly recommended film, suitable not only for young children, but also for older students, and adults. Each age group gets different understandings from it, and finds subtle nuances of simple to complex ideas that have to do with creation, differences, similarities, wall-building, brotherhood, and cooperation. Endorsed by the Family Service Corporation. Color. 15 minutes. Source: Contemporary Films.

FILMSTRIPS

PREJUDICES AND STEREOTYPES:

Maple Street All-Americans

The boys who live on the same street in a typical town discover that they can have more fun and better teams by choosing playmates without regard for their names, skin, color, or church. Cartoon story. With script. 42 frames. Philadelphia Friendship Council.

The Rabbit Brothers

Humorous cartoon showing that color has nothing to do with character, and that liking and disliking others should be based on individual merits. Captions. 34 frames. Source: Anti-Defamation League.

WORLD FRIENDS:

A Garden We Planted Together

Stresses the value of cooperative projects if success is to be expected. Also emphasizes necessity for international understanding. Color. 35 frames. Source: United Nations. (Book available by same title.)

Growing as World Friends

Illustrates expanding concepts of friendship from smaller areas to larger areas to world friends. Color. Source: Friendship Press.

FOR JUNIOR HIGH SCHOOL STUDENTS

FILMS

ANTI-SEMITISM:

An American Girl

This film is based on an actual event, and tells the story of an American teen-ager who is mistakenly labeled Jewish by friends and neighbors. The theme revolves around anti-Semitism, but is basically concerned with irrational, unsocial prejudice and stereo-typing. A very fine discussion catalyst. 30 minutes. Source: Jew-ish Community Relations Council.

Anti-Semitism in America

A Professor of Sociology and Anthropology at Princeton Univer-sity, Dr. Melvin Tumin, presents a depth-study of attitudes and motivations underlying anti-Semitism, and places special empha-sis on less overt types of prejudiced persons. 25 minutes. Source: Anti-Defamation League.

CBS "FYI" Series

There are many fine CBS films that highlight current social issues, economic plights of various groups, and racial discrimina-tion. These are worth investigating, and are being made con-stantly. This particular film is a kinescope dealing with anti-Semitic vandalism and the desecration of places of worship. Arnold Forster, ADL General Counsel, analyzes the motivation and character of the incidents. Discussion-starter, and very good for talking about other analogies involving race and religion. 29 minutes. Source: Anti-Defamation League.

Remember Us

A documentary of the Nazi atrocities. Firsthand reports are given by several survivors who now live in the United States concerning their experiences under the Nazi regime. 60 minutes. Source: Anti-Defamation League.

DISCRIMINATION AND SEGREGATION:

Cast the First Stone

Narrated by John Daly, this documentary, originally shown on ABC-TV, features interviews with Americans whose lives have been affected by prejudice: Negroes in Los Angeles and Chicago; Jews in Detroit; Puerto Ricans in New York; Mexicans, Japanese, and Chinese in the Midwest—these people describe their experi-ences and discuss their outlook for the future. 42 minutes. Source: Anti-Defamation League.

The Challenge

This is a prize-winning *March of Time* film. It follows a writer-photographer team doing a series of articles on Civil Rights. Across the United States they interview church, business and labor leaders, observe examples of discrimination, and locate groups working to safeguard Civil Rights programs. 30 minutes. Source: Jewish Community Relations Council.

To Live Together

This interracial camp episode is a sensitive documentary, treating the camp experience and its effect on attitudes through the use of spontaneous and unrehearsed questions and thoughts about race. 35 minutes. Source: Philadelphia Friendship Council.

NBC White Paper on Sit-Ins

This documentary of the NBC "White Paper" series on the sit-in movement in southern U.S. is a dramatic portrayal of young Negro college students demanding human and civil rights. 60 minutes. Source: Anti-Defamation League.

Report from Alabama

This is a kinescope of the special NBC telecast on the U.S. Civil Rights Commission hearings in Montgomery, Alabama. It is devoted to investigation of the charges of denial of voting rights in that state. 30 minutes. Source: Anti-Defamation League.

The Story of Sammy Lee

This documentary of the "Confidential File" TV series illustrates the fact that many unprejudiced children grow up to discriminate and to be discriminated against; a comparison is made with those who grow up with happy experiences of living and working in prejudice-free atmospheres. 30 minutes. Source: Anti-Defamation League and Philadelphia Friendship Council.

Sydenham Plan

Narrated by José Ferrer, this is an account of the work being done in America's first interracial hospital in which Negro and white staff members serve together to relieve suffering of all groups. 10 minutes. Source: Philadelphia Friendship Council.

FAIR EMPLOYMENT PRACTICES:

Burden of Truth

An important theme that highlights the plight of the American who is of a different skin color as he seeks a decent job and home for himself and his family. Produced by the United Steelworkers of America, Committee on Civil Rights. Teacher's manual and stu-

dent discussion guides. 43 or 67 minutes. Source: United Steelworkers, and others.

For Fair Play

Two fathers with a common problem come together to offer more
than lip service to mutual cooperation for equal opportunity. Reveals how it feels to experience discrimination. 27 minutes. Source:
American Friends Service Committee.

A Morning for Jimmy

School discouragement results from personal and family experience with discrimination. Jimmy's teachers and several friends help
to persuade him of the importance of education for better life
preparation. Encourages good discussion of the effects of prejudice
on motivation, and the influence of understanding adults and
friends in raising aspiration levels. 28 minutes. Source: National
Urban League.

The New Girl

The story of the first Negro girl hired in the office of a manufac-
turer dramatizes the fears of management, other employees, and
the applicant concerning the new job. Effective techniques of integration in employment are emphasized. Produced by the President's Committee on Government Contracts. 30 minutes. Source:
Human Relations Council, and Anti-Defamation League.

FAIR HOUSING PRACTICES:

For White Christians Only

This is a kinescope of NBC's National Educational Television program on discrimination in housing—specifically against Negroes
and Jews. There is a round-table discussion with three experts, and
Jackie Robinson describes his house-hunting experiences. A real
estate broker from Fairfield County, Connecticut, explains how
housing discrimination against Jews operates in his area. 30 minutes. Source: Anti-Defamation League.

IMMIGRANTS, NEWCOMERS, AND IMMIGRATION:

The Golden Door

A cartoon film that examines current laws and proposals for improving immigration legislation. Color. 15 minutes. Source: Anti-
Defamation League.

INTERNATIONAL HUMAN RIGHTS:

Of Human Rights

Illustrates the importance and the meaning of the United Nations' Universal Declaration of Human Rights to all people at home and abroad. 21 minutes. Source: National Council of Christians and Jews.

Our Town Is the World

Also concentrated on the implications of the United Nations' Declaration of Human Rights. Emphasizes equal rights to accept and respect all people. 10 minutes. Source: Philadelphia Friendship Council.

Which Way for Human Rights?

Discussion-starter concerning who should enforce the Universal Declaration of Human Rights, and whether violations are punishable—if so, by whom? 9 minutes. Source: Anti-Defamation League.

INTERRELIGIOUS UNDERSTANDING:

Major Religions of the World

Animated diagrams illustrate rise of new religions from older ones, and illustrate the beliefs and important rituals of Hinduism, Buddhism, Judaism, Christianity, and Islam. Color. 20 minutes. Source: Encyclopaedia Britannica Films.

NEGRO-AMERICANS:

Booker T. Washington

Narrates and reproduces episodes that illustrate this great Negro's struggle to free his fellow Negroes from poverty, fear, and ignorance. 18 minutes. Source: Encyclopaedia Britannica Films.

Lady From Philadelphia

Marian Anderson's "See It Now" (CBS) tour filmed while she was an ambassador of good will in Asiatic countries. She discusses U.S. policies, personal experiences, and world affairs in interviews and informal exchanges. Her philosophy of life is a model for all people. 60 minutes. Source: Contemporary Films.

Story of Dr. Carver

This Metro-Goldwyn-Mayer film tells the story of how a Negro slave grew to be a great teacher and scientist. 11 minutes. Source: American Federation of Labor-CIO (AFL-CIO).

The American Jew: A Tribute to Freedom

Produced by CBS television in cooperation with the Anti-Defamation League, this kinescope film shows the contributions of American Jews to this country's heritage. Jeff Chandler is the narrator, and he is assisted by Senator Herbert H. Lehman, Richard Tucker, Dore Schary, Susan Strasberg, and others. 25 minutes. Source: Anti-Defamation League.

A Girl from Puerto Rico

Depicts the activities and actions of a social studies class in helping to increase understanding towards Puerto Ricans entering the city schools in New York City. Color. 20 minutes. Source: National Council of Public Relations.

Sons of Liberty

Haym Solomon's life during Revolutionary War times; participation in the "Sons of Liberty" movement; capture and imprisonment by British soldiers; fund-raising activities for the Continental Army. Color. 20 minutes. Source: United Artists Association.

A Way in The Wilderness

Dr. Joseph Goldberger of the U.S. Public Health Service conquers pellagra. 11 minutes. Source: Teaching Film Custodians.

PREJUDICE AND STEREOTYPES:

Boundary Lines

The boundary lines are illustrated as nationality, religion, and color—these divide people. A plea is made for elimination of these lines. 11 minutes. Source: Jewish Community Relations Council, and others.

The High Wall

Saturday Review's guide to films said of this film: *"The High Wall* comes the closest of any film yet made to actually showing some of the basic origins and meanings of prejudice." This prize-winning film shows how the teen-ager's hostility toward people of other religions, nationality, and racial groups is a product of the frustrations and prejudices of his parents. 30 minutes. Source: Council of Human Relations.

Picture in Your Mind

An animated film that won the award of the United Nations Film Board for the contribution it makes to the concepts of world unity. Excellent for stimulating discussion about the causes and effects of prejudice. 16 minutes. Source: Anti-Defamation League.

Rumor

Case history of a rumor that caused conflict and tension; suggests discussion about rumors and each person's responsibility to help stop them from spreading. 8 minutes. Source: Anti-Defamation League.

Rumor Clinic

National ADL Director Benjamin Epstein conducts a "Rumor Clinic" on NBC's "Home Show." Included are the "Home Show" cast: Arlene Francis, Hugh Downs, and Howard Whitman. 24 minutes. Source: Anti-Defamation League.

PROJECTS FOR BROTHERHOOD AND INTERGROUP EDUCATION:

Make Way for Youth

Produced in cooperation with the Youth Division of the National Social Welfare Assembly, and narrated by Melvyn Douglas, this film shows the people of Madison, Wisconsin, cooperating to organize a youth council that built understanding among races, religions, and neighborhoods. 22 minutes. Source: Jewish Community Relations Council.

Racial Differences

Presents scientific discoveries and theories concerning the skin color differences of man, and illustrates the physiological, genetic, and geographic conditions that cause differences. Color. 10 minutes. AFL-CIO.

FILMSTRIPS

DISCRIMINATION AND SEGREGATION:

Forward—All Together

Origins and sequences of denial of rights to minority groups are illustrated in this filmstrip, and suggestions are made concerning antidotes and actions to help unlearn stereotypes and support equal rights. With script. 82 frames. Source: Philadelphia Friendship Council.

Let's Live Democracy

Happiness and freedom are dependent upon everyone's acceptance of the tenet of opportunity for all. With recording. 18 minutes. Source: Philadelphia Friendship Council.

Man—One Family

Illustrated realities of race, religion, and nationality, emphasizing the facts that none of these determine man's abilities and that all are equal and worthy of equal opportunity. With script. 57 frames. Source: Jewish Community Relations Council.

The Spiral of Social Change

Based on the book, *One Nation,* by Wallace Stegner and the editors of *Look* magazine, this filmstrip illustrates ways that discrimination causes delinquency, sickness, and ignorance. With script. 44 frames. Source: National Council of Christians and Jews.

FAIR EMPLOYMENT PRACTICES:

Workers for Equality

Explains why and how the United Steelworkers, CIO, and AFL have worked for nondiscrimination in hiring. With 15-minute recording. 37 frames. Source: Jewish Labor Committee.

INTERRELIGIOUS UNDERSTANDING:

American Religious Holidays

America has a Judaic-Christian heritage, and the significance of religious rituals and experiences in the Jewish and Christian faiths is illustrated here. With script. 50 frames. Source: Anti-Defamation League.

One God

The three major religious faiths in America, Catholic, Protestant, and Jewish, and the ways of worship of these groups. Based on the film and book of the same title. With script and/or record. 100 frames. Source: Anti-Defamation League.

There is also another film on these same subjects called *The Ways We Worship In America,* and based on the film *One God.* These are available from the National Council of Christians and Jews. Series consists of:

One God—With script of 33⅓ r.p.m. recording. 100 frames.
The Protestant Way—With script. 71 frames.
The Catholic Way—With script. 64 frames.
The Jewish Way—With script. 70 frames.

The World's Great Religions

Documentaries based on the *Life* magazine series. Color, with captions and script. Source: Encyclopaedia Britannica Films. Consists of:

Hinduism—77 frames   *Islam*—79 frames
Buddhism—71 frames   *Judaism*—74 frames
Confucianism and Taoism—64 frames   *Christianity*—85 frames

NEGRO-AMERICANS:

The American Negro

Based on the book *One Nation* by Wallace Stegner and the editors of *Look* magazine. This is a fine documentary about what it is like to be a Negro in America, and the achievements of Negroes. The challenge of ending discrimination is emphasized. With script. 49 frames. Source: National Conference of Christians and Jews.

OTHER MINORITY GROUPS IN AMERICAN LIFE:

Early Americans

History and development of problems for groups such as Indian, Mexican, and Spanish Americans and efforts to solve them. Also based on the book *One Nation* by Wallace Stegner and the editors of *Look* magazine. With script. 47 frames. Source: National Conference of Christians and Jews.

Pacific Races

Chinese, Japanese, and Filipino Americans have been victims of prejudice and discrimination in American life. This film, based on the book *One Nation* by Wallace Stegner and the editors of *Look* magazine, discusses lives and problems of these groups in America. With script. 47 frames. Source: Philadelphia Friendship Council, and National Conference of Christians and Jews.

300 Years

Highlights and memorable events in the history of Jewish people in America. With script. Source: Jewish Community Relations Council.

PREJUDICE AND STEREOTYPES:

Free To Be Different

Challenges Americans to appreciate cultural and religious differences in a country like this one that has been dedicated to freedom and cooperative free enterprise. Based on the book *American Counterpoint* by Alexander Alland and Pearl Buck. With script. 50 frames. Source: Anti-Defamation League and National Conference of Christians and Jews.

None so Blind

Details the origin and history of prejudice from early childhood through adulthood, and discusses what individuals can do to overcome harmful dislikes. Comes with 13-minute recording, captions or script, and discussion guide. 57 frames. Source: National Conference of Christians and Jews and Anti-Defamation League.

Rumor Clinic

Gordon Allport, the noted Harvard psychologist whose studies have been cited in this book, developed this game that involves people in lively discussion and self-teaching demonstrations portraying how we all have stereotypes and prejudices that distort what we hear and see, and cause harmful rumors to be initiated and perpetuated. 3 frames. Source: Jewish Labor Council and others.

FOR SENIOR HIGH SCHOOL STUDENTS AND ADULTS

FILMS

CITIES TODAY:

The City: A Second Chance and *A Chance at the Beginning*

Dr. Martin Deutsch, Director of the Institute of Developmental Studies, Department of Psychiatry at New York Medical College, with a staff of trained social workers and teachers, engages in experimental pre-kindergarten work to meet the needs of four-year-old slum children. Source: Anti-Defamation League.

No Hiding Place

This film, originally produced for CBS television series "East Side, West Side," depicts exploitations by unethical real estate dealers of a Negro family that had moved into a formerly all-white neighborhood. Discussion guide. 45 minutes. Source: Anti-Defamation League.

DISCRIMINATION AND SEGREGATION:

Segregation in the Schools

Edward R. Murrow's "See It Now" television discussion of Supreme Court rulings on school segregation. Shows reactions of Negro and white students, teachers, ministers, and civic leaders in two Southern communities. 25 minutes. AFL-CIO.

Walk to Freedom

This is a newsreel-type film of the now historic Montgomery, Alabama, bus boycott, and the role of nonviolence in achieving social progress. 20 minutes. Source: American Friends Service Committee.

FAIR EMPLOYMENT PRACTICES:

The Case of Mary Doe

Members of the staff and Commissioners of the Pittsburgh, Pennsylvania, Fair Employment Practice Commission (later called the Commission on Human Relations) show how employment cases are handled by the Commission through the reenactment of the case of Mary Doe. All steps in the process are shown from the filing of a complaint through investigation, conciliation, and final determination of the case. 28 minutes. Source: Council of Human Relations.

Chuck Hansen—One Guy

Corporations such as General Cable and General Electric achieved increased production, less absenteeism, and better plant morale by successfully applying an approach they called "Team Work in Industry." This policy concerned an approach to the problems of prejudice and discrimination among their employees. The film and the project were sponsored by the Labor-Management Commission of the National Conference of Christians and Jews. Color. 26 minutes. Source: National Conference of Christians and Jews, and others.

Commencement

The President's Committee on Government Contracts' story of an employer's failure to make his policy of employment on merit clear, and the resulting boycott of talent when his subordinates and employment referral agencies assumed that minority workers were not wanted in his organization. Demonstrates the company's deprivation of some of the best qualified workers it might have had. 20 minutes. Source: Council of Human Relations, and others.

Joe Davis, American

An honors college graduate, Joe Davis experiences employment discrimination because he is a Negro, even though he has an engineering degree. Senator Wayne Morris and a spokesman for the CIO discuss the problem, and explain their support for the federal fair employment practices law. 13 minutes. Source: AFL-CIO.

FAIR HOUSING PRACTICES:

All the Way Home

As a Negro American family looks at a house in an all-white neighborhood, the film shows the fears and ill-disguised attitudes of the seller, neighbors, real estate broker, and minister. A challenge is given to the viewer to decide what his responsibilities would have been in this situation. 30 minutes. Council on Human Relations, Anti-Defamation League, and others.

Crisis in Levittown

Professor Dan Dodson, Director of the Center for Human Relations and Community Studies, offers comment and analysis after a series of interviews with residents who are for or against the first Negro family to move into Levittown, Pennsylvania. 32 minutes. Source: Council of Human Relations, Anti-Defamation League, and others.

In Search of Housing

A Negro engineer seeks decent housing near his work; his problems and the meanings of the problem to his employer are well illustrated here. The enforcement of a fair housing practices law and how it solved this particular problem are shown. Produced by the New York State Commission Against Discrimination. 12 minutes. Source: Human Relations Council.

IMMIGRANTS, NEWCOMERS, AND IMMIGRATION:

New Americans

Documents the contributions of immigrants from other nations to America, and criticizes the McCarran Immigration Act as a discriminatory policy. 20 minutes. Source: Philadelphia Friendship Council.

Passport to Nowhere

RKO made this highly rated film on displaced persons, and uses the technique of dramatic presentation through actual case histories. 20 minutes. Source: Philadelphia Friendship Council.

INTERGROUP EDUCATION IN SCHOOLS:

Challenge to America

Professor William Van Til, Chairman of the Department of Secondary Education at New York University, illustrates the role of education in effective intergroup relations. Ways and means of meeting the challenge of effecting better human relations among people of various religious, racial, and nationality backgrounds are illustrated and discussed. 25 minutes. Source: Anti-Defamation League.

Challenge to American Education: A Question of Chairs

Traces the development of American education from its early colonial beginnings to the present. Produced in cooperation with CBS. 45 minutes. Source: Anti-Defamation League.

The Chosen People

A group of teen-agers who are planning a class prom discover that their club has an unwritten "gentleman's agreement" that excludes Jewish students, and they do something about it! Discussion guide. 27 minutes. Source: Anti-Defamation League and others.

Make Way for Youth

This story of how a group of teen-agers shelved racial prejudice in favor of cooperative recreational and civic projects should be seen and discussed by students, teachers, and other adults responsible for directing the affairs of young people. Self-direction and channeling of both energies and prejudices can be the desirable end result. 32 minutes. Anti-Defamation League.

NEGRO AMERICANS:

Epitaph for Jim Crow

This consists of a *series of five one-half hour long* illustrated film-lectures on the Negro American narrated by Dr. Thomas Pettigrew of Harvard University. This eminent scholar discusses the history and current changes in race relations in America. 5 films in series. One half-hour each. Source: Anti-Defamation League.

Salute to the American Theatre

Illustrates the important influence of the theatre as a force in the fight against prejudice and discrimination. Talented actors and actresses present scenes from plays such as *The Male Animal, Home of the Brave, The Crucible,* and *A Raisin in the Sun.* Produced in cooperation with CBS. 45 minutes. Source: Anti-Defamation League.

PREJUDICES AND STEREOTYPES:

An American Girl

This film is based on the true story of how one American girl experienced the effects of prejudice and the great harm it can do. 29 minutes. Source: Anti-Defamation League.

Broken Mask

The story of two young college students, one a Negro, who have to come to grips with man-made barriers of skin-color prejudice. Through their experiences, they come to realize and demonstrate that being able to live together harmoniously in spite of outside pressures is a challenge for everyone. 29 minutes. Source: Broadcasting and Film Corporation.

Can We Immunize Against Prejudice?

This animated-drawing film shows three ways some parents have attempted to help their children grow up free of prejudice. Limited success is experienced in each example, and discussion is engendered about what possibilities there are for parents and other adults to help educate for immunization against prejudice. 7 minutes. Source: National Council of Christians and Jews, and others.

The High Wall

A case study of a young bigot, describing how he became infected with bigotry and how his home life fostered the development of prejudice. Discussion guide. 32 minutes. Source: AFL-CIO and others.

he Man Who Knows It All

Dr. Irving J. Lee of Northwestern University stresses the need to communicate accurately for better understanding, and the development of know-it-all attitudes that hinder learning and lead to intergroup tension and bigotry. 30 minutes. Source: American Friends Service Committee.

Tragedy in a Temporary Town

Kinescope of an NBC program by Reginald Rose, starring Lloyd Bridges. This is an account of what can occur at a temporary construction workers' camp when a rumor causes an innocent victim to be accused of a crime he did not commit. Ensuing hysteria that illustrates blind prejudice against a minority group erupts. This film won an Anti-Defamation League Television Award. 48 minutes. Source: Anti-Defamation League.

Unlearning Prejudice

This is a kinescope from the NBC "Open Mind" series. Panel discussion of various aspects of antisocial prejudice by panelists Benjamin Epstein, ADL National Director, Elmo Roper, Public Opinion Analyst, and Marie Johoda, New York University Professor of Psychology. 30 minutes. Source: Anti-Defamation League.

Wanted—A Place to Live

This film is especially designed to provoke discussion on prejudices and their effects on people. 15 minutes. Source: Anti-Defamation League.

RACIAL DIFFERENCES:

Common Fallacies About Group Differences

Using a script prepared by Professor Clifford Morgan of Johns Hopkins University, this film begins with valid and modern interpretations of the truths and fallacies about race, and exposes common errors. It shows graphically that group behavioral differences are the result of the culture in which one grows up rather than heredity, and illustrates the fact that the behavior of one person should not cause people to generalize about the people of the entire group. 15 minutes. Source: Jewish Community Relations Council.

FILMSTRIPS

The following are representative of filmstrips that can be located through the associations cited as good sources of visual materials. Included here are materials that have to do with fair employment practices, fair housing practices, projects for brotherhood, and the rise and fall of racial supremacy ideologies.

Anatomy of Nazism

Historical, social, cultural, economic, and political workings of fascism in Hitler's Germany, and the threat to democracy of totalitarianism. 53 frames. Color. Source: Anti-Defamation League.

It's Good Business

This was produced by the Illinois State Chamber of Commerce for businessmen's audiences as part of the Chamber's educational program for equal job opportunities. Shows factually why and how management should start hiring on merit. With 33⅓ r.p.m. record. 34 minutes. Source: Council of Human Relations.

It's up to You

Illustrates the tools and programs that the individual and groups can use to help replace intolerance with cooperation and unity. With script. 30 frames. Source: Council of Human Relations.

Something to Work for

Automation and discrimination require both preparation for employment at one's highest skill levels and the use of fair employment practice laws. This film also stresses the role of parents in the vocational guidance of their children. Produced by the Philadelphia Commission on Human Relations. With tape recording. 25 minutes. Source: Council on Human Relations.

The Good Neighbor

Community leaders have a great responsibility to promote fair housing opportunities, and the practical suggestions offered here for both individual and group activities in this direction are emphasized in this film. Ths was also produced by the Philadelphia Commission on Human Relations. With tape recording. Also available with 33⅓ r.p.m. record. Source: Commission on Human Relations.

The House Across the Street

Illustrates ways neighbors and a neighborhood can react cooperatively and constructively when Negroes, or other "different" families move into a neighborhood. With tape recording, or 33⅓ r.p.m. record. Source: Commission on Human Relations, Anti-Defamation League, and others.

The House of Decision

This persuades Negro families to seek housing outside of the ghettoes and slums, and focuses on the anti-discrimination commission. Produced by the Philadelphia Commission on Human Relations. With tape recording, or 33⅓ r.p.m. record. 25 minutes. Source: Commission on Human Relations.

To Secure These Rights

This illustrates the recommendations of the President's Committee on Civil Rights concerning education and legislation to secure equal opportunity. With script. 50 frames. Source: Anti-Defamation League and National Conference of Christians and Jews.

We Live in Peace

Scenes of activities in Los Angeles' Aliso Housing Project for Negro, Oriental, Mexican, and Anglo-American families demonstrating the thesis that meeting and working and living together lead to friendship and understanding among those who are neighbors. With captions. 60 frames. Source: Anti-Defamation League and Jewish Community Relations Council.

BOOKS WITH INTERGROUP EDUCATION THEMES

FOR PRIMARY AND MIDDLE SCHOOL CHILDREN

This list of suggestions is by no means complete and intends only to suggest some types of books that adults may use with children and that can be used to guide children in self-selection. Included are some books of music, games, stories, plays, and poems. Some books are annotated, and many have self-explanatory titles. The reading process itself will be highly motivated and encouraged by the kind of books which help children relate realistically to other children of differing races, creeds, and nationalities. An attempt is made here to give *approximate* recommended usage level, although many books that cannot be read *by* children can be used for reading *to* children. Long after children can read independently, there is an important place for well-read stories by adults in the group living of parents and children and of teachers and children. *Primary* is here used to designate children from four years of age through approximately grade four. *Upper Elementary* is used to designate those more suitable because of content to boys and girls in grades four through eight.

Angelo, Valenti, *Big Little Island:* A war orphan learns to feel at home among the Italian-Americans of Manhattan. New York, Viking Press, Inc. (Upper Elementary)

Angelo, Valenti, *Hill of Little Miracles:* A story of Italian life in San Francisco—told with humor and kindness. New York, Viking Press, Inc. (Upper Elementary)

Anglund, Joan W., *A Friend Is Someone Who Likes You:* Rhymes and pictures about friendship. New York, Harcourt, Brace & Company, Inc. (Primary)

Ayer, Jacqueline, *Nudang and His Kite:* A Siamese boy meets many different types of people in his community as he searches for his lost kite. New York, Harcourt, Brace & Company, Inc. (Primary)

Baugh, Dolores M., and Pulsifer, Marjorie P., *Chandler Language Experience Readers* with accompanying films (several titles) for beginning readers. San Francisco. Chandler Publishing Company.

Beim, Jerrold, *Swimming Hole:* A picture-story book that cleverly ridicules color prejudice in ways that the youngest child can understand. New York, William Morrow & Company. (Primary)

Beim, Jerrold, *The Smallest Boy in the Class:* Useful for illustrating peer relationships and individual worth. New York, William Morrow & Company. (Primary)

Beim, Jerrold and Lorraine, *Two Is a Team:* Ted and Paul, Negro and white friends, differ on the best way to build a coaster and decide on pooling their ideas. New York, Harcourt, Brace & Company, Inc. (Primary)

Beskow, Elsa, *Pella's New Suit:* This ever-popular story is set in Sweden, and stresses cooperative living and interdependence of families and neighbors. New York, Harper and Brothers. (Primary)

Bishop, Claire Huchet, *All Alone:* Two boys tending herds in the French Alps break the community "keep-it-to-yourself" rule, and near disaster follows. But the way of life in the community is improved. New York, Viking Press, Inc. (Primary)

Bishop, Claire Huchet, *Paris Pancakes:* A war-torn French family undergoes much disaster but remains courageous and valiant. New York, Viking Press, Inc. (Primary)

Bishop, Claire Huchet, *Twenty and Ten:* During Nazi occupation of France, 20 French children are taken to a refuge by a wise friend. Hiding and saving the children is a tale of courage and caring. New York, Viking Press, Inc. (Upper Elementary)

Black, Irma Simonton, and others, *The Bank Street Readers:* Excellent books for beginning reading—more realistic vocabulary and illustrations. Several titles. New York, The Macmillan Co.

Bontemps, Arna, *Frederick Douglass,* New York, Alfred A. Knopf, Inc. (Upper Elementary)

Bontemps, Arna, *Sad Faced Boy:* Three Negro boys from Alabama find exciting adventures and contrasts when they visit Harlem and see the sights of New York City. Boston, Houghton Mifflin Co. (Upper Elementary)

Bontemps, Arna, *Story of the Negro:* A brief history highlighting key problems, issues, and people. New York, Alfred A. Knopf, Inc. (Upper Elementary)

Brenner, Barbara, *Barto Takes the Subway:* A city child has new adventures and meets many kinds of neighbors in New York City. New York, Alfred A. Knopf, Inc. (Primary)

Brown, Jeanette Perkins, *Ronnie's Wish:* A small Negro boy has interesting adventures in the children's zoo. New York, Friendship Press. (Primary)

Bulla, Clyde Robert, *The Poppy Seeds:* Pablo brings water, flowers, and happiness to his Mexican Valley when he persuades rich, selfish Antonio to share his water supply with neighbors. New York, Crowell-Collier Publishing Co. (Primary)

Carlson, Natalie, *A Brother for the Orphelines:* The Orphelines manage to find a way to keep a baby boy left on their doorstep, and warm human relationships develop. New York, Harper and Brothers. (Upper Elementary as well as Primary)

Carlson, Natalie, *Family Under the Bridge:* Happiness for a French family that is loyal in the midst of deprivation. New York, Harper and Brothers. (Primary and older)

Carlson, Natalie, *Tomahawk Valley:* Two present-day Indian children cope with a stubborn grandmother. New York, Harper and Brothers. (Primary and Upper Elementary)

Chu, Daniel and Skinner, *A Glorious Age in Africa:* Designed to engender understanding and pride in African culture and heritage. Garden City, Doubleday and Company, Inc. (Upper Elementary)

Credle, Ellis, *Down, Down the Mountain:* Earning money to buy new shoes becomes a family project in a log cabin in the Blue Ridge mountains. New York, Thomas Nelson & Sons. (Primary and Upper Elementary)

Dagliesch, Alice, *Courage of Sarah Noble:* A puritan child's loneliness, hard work, and meetings with strange new neighbors help her develop insight and courage. New York, Charles Scribner's Sons. (Upper Elementary)

Daniel, Anita, *The Story of Albert Schweitzer:* Well-written biography of the work and ideals of this great man who gives himself to the service of mankind and puts into practice what many people only preach. New York, Random House, Inc. (Upper Elementary)

Di Angeli, Marguerite, *Bright April:* Because of her happy home, love of school, and being a Brownie Scout, "little brown April" is usually Bright April. Kindness, cooperation, and loving understanding pervade this and the following Di Angeli stories. Garden City, Doubleday & Company, Inc. (Primary and Upper Elementary)

Di Angeli, Marguerite, *Thee Hannah:* A little Quaker girl uses her bonnet to help a slave and her child. Garden City, Doubleday & Company, Inc. (Primary and Upper Elementary)

Di Angeli, *Skippack School:* A Mennonite child attends school for the first time and learns from others about others. Garden City, Doubleday & Company, Inc. (Primary and Upper Elementary)

DuBois, William Pene, *Bear Party:* Koala Bears play happily until the fact that they are identical causes grievances and quarreling. Masks save the day. New York, Viking Press, Inc. (For children of all ages)

DuBois, William Pene, *The Three Policemen:* Stories of tall tales and development of recognition of differences, cooperation, and intelligent action. New York, Viking Press, Inc. (All ages)

Emblem, Don and Betty, *The Palomino Boy:* A Mexican orphan in California discounts discrimination against him when he realizes that brown skin does not make him inferior any more than black, brown, or white color makes one of his horses better than another. New York, Viking Press, Inc. (Upper Elementary)

Estes, Eleanor, *The Hundred Dresses:* The pathos of human relationships and suffering of those who are different from the local majority are described simply and beautifully in this story of

Wanda, a little Polish girl, who did not "belong." New York, Harcourt, Brace & Company, Inc. (Upper Elementary)

Evans, Eva Knox, *All about Us,* and sequel, *People Are Important:* Very effective presentations of scientific facts about people in group relationships that help combat intolerance and prejudice. New York, Capitol Publishing Co. (Upper Elementary)

Faulkner, Georgene, *Melindy's Happy Summer:* Summer vacation exchange of Negroes in big cities with white children from the country. Sensitively handled. New York, Julian Messner, Inc. (All ages)

Faulkner, Georgene, *Melindy's Medal:* A story about a middle-class family in a Boston housing development, and a sequel to the first book. Julian Messner, Inc. (All ages)

Felt, Sue, *Rosa-Too-Little:* An Italian-American neighborhood in New York City is the setting for this story about Rosa who is too young for the Library but longs to belong. Garden City, Doubleday & Company, Inc. (Primary)

Fisher, Aileen, *A Lantern in the Window:* Peter goes to live with Quaker relatives in pre–Civil War times, and learns that the farm is a station on the underground railroad. New York, Thomas Nelson & Sons. (Upper Elementary)

Fitch, Florence, *One God:* An objective and reverent book describing the ways of Catholics, Jews, and Protestants that should contribute to better understanding of all religions and qualities of living. New York, Lothrop, Lee and Shepard Co. (Upper Elementary)

Friedman, Frieda, *A Sundae with Judy:* Interracial families cooperate in a financial crisis and save the day through their children. New York, William Morrow & Company. (All ages)

Hagler, Margaret, *Larry and the Freedom Man:* A twelve-year-old white boy and his uncle help Daniel, a slave boy, and his family gain freedom when they meet on a trip to Kansas. New York, Lothrop, Lee and Shepard Co. (Upper Elementary)

Hastings, Florence, *Skid:* Skid's family moves from a small town in Georgia to live with an aunt in Connecticut. As the only Negro family in an exclusive white community, Skid and his family face the feelings and actions of other children about teams, scholastic honors, and success in after-school activities. Boston, Houghton Mifflin Co. (Upper Elementary)

Hogan, Inez, *Happy Has a New Friend:* Illustrations present excellent intergroup images in this simple story about friendship. New York, E. P. Dutton & Co., Inc. (Primary)

Hughes, Langston, *The Dream Keeper:* "The Dreamkeeper and Other Poems" by this gifted author is also available in a recording made by Mr. Hughes. Book by Alfred A. Knopf, Inc., New York. Records by Folkways. (Upper Elementary)

Hughes, Langston, *Pictorial History of the Negro in America:* New York, Crown Publishers, Inc., and *Negro in America,* New York, Dodd, Mead & Company. (Upper Elementary)

Hughes, Langston, and Bontemps, Arna, *The Book of Negro Folklore:* An exclusive collection—song, story, and poetry—representing the rich contribution to American literature and folk expression of the Negro from slavery to this era of jazz and jive. New York, Dodd, Mead & Company, Inc. (Upper Elementary)

Ipcar, Dahlov, *Black and White:* New York, Alfred A. Knopf, Inc. (Upper Elementary)

Ish-Kisher, *A Boy of Old Prague:* New York, Pantheon Books, Inc. (Upper Elementary)

Jackson, Jesse, *Call Me Charlie:* The only Negro boy in his school, Charlie had to use patience and his other best qualities to achieve acceptance in the community. New York, Harper and Brothers. (Upper Elementary)

Jones, Ruth Fosdick, *Escape to Freedom:* Using actual adventures of her grandparents, the author weaves a lively story about the adventures of two boys who join in the excitement of operating a station on the underground railroad in Civil War days. New York, Random House, Inc. (Upper Elementary)

Justis, May, *New Boy in School:* Locale is an integrated Tennessee school and the story concerns a Negro boy, the first in an all-white classroom. New York, Hastings House Publishers, Inc. (Upper Elementary)

Kelly, Regina Z., *Lincoln and Douglas,* New York, Random House, Inc. (Upper Elementary)

Kraus, Robert, *The Rabbit Brothers:* A humorous cartoon booklet about twin rabbits and their different reactions to rabbits unlike themselves—one dislikes them and is miserable; the other tries to find some good in all rabbits, and he is much happier than his friend. Anti-Defamation League. (All ages)

Krauss, Ruth, *I'll Be You and You Be Me:* A book about feelings, friendship, love, and belonging. New York, Harper and Brothers. (All ages)

Krumgold, Joseph, *And Now Miguel:* Miguel longs to prove himself and works as a shepherd on a farm near Taos, Mexico. His problems with human relationships help children understand themselves better. New York, Crowell-Collier Publishing Co. (All ages)

Leaf, Monroe, *Three Promises to You:* Phrases and drawings help boys and girls understand what the United Nations is and what it does. Philadelphia, J. B. Lippincott Company. (All ages)

Lenski, Lois, *Strawberry Girl:* Conrtasts the lives of an industrious family and those of a shiftless family who are neighbors in Florida. The friendly, ambitious family helps the Slaters adopt thrifty ways. Philadelphia, J. B. Lippincott Company. (All ages)

Lionni, Leo, *Swimmy:* One little black fish saves the lives of a group of fellow baby fish. New York, Pantheon Books, Inc. (Primary and up)

Lerner, Marguerite Rush, *Red Man, White Man, African Chief:* Won the 1961 Brotherhood Award, and explains skin pigmentation to children in familiar terms and uses familiar analogies. Minneapolis, Medical Books for Children. (All ages)

Lewiton, Mina, *Candita's Choice:* A little Puerto Rican girl's gradual adjustments to life in chilly, crowded New York City (for her). A frank portrayal of difficulties faced by Puerto Rican arrivals to the city. New York, Harper and Brothers. (Upper Elementary)

McNeer, May, *Armed With Courage:* Biographies of seven dedicated men and women who worked in science, religion, or social work for the betterment of mankind. New York, Abingdon Press. (Upper Elementary)

Means, Florence Crannell, *A Great Day in the Morning:* A Negro girl experiences the bitterness of racial prejudice but has the courage to continue. At Tuskegee, she comes to know Dr. Carver, and decides to become a nurse. Boston, Houghton Mifflin Company. (Upper Elementary)

Millen, Nina, *Children's Games from Many Lands:* 262 games from 55 different lands with easy to follow directions. New York, Friendship Press. (All ages)

Ormsby, Virginia, *Twenty-one Children:* The story of a new Puerto Rican child in kindergarten is handled with simplicity and feeling. Philadelphia, J. B. Lippincott Company. (Primary)

Politi, Leo, *Juanita:* A charming story of the Latin Americans who live on Olvera Street in Los Angeles. New York, Charles Scribner's Sons. (Upper Elementary)

Randall, Blossom, *Fun for Chris:* A picture-story book that gives the reasons for different skin colors. New York, Albert Whitman & Co. (All ages, particularly Primary)

Scherman, Katherine, *The Slave Who Freed Haiti:* New York, Random House, Inc. (Upper Elementary and older students)

Keckar, Alvena, *Zusks of the Burning Hills:* Zusks, born of Czechoslovakian parents, experiences hard times with her family in the coal fields of a mining country. New York, Henry Z. Walck. (Upper Elementary)

Seuss, Dr., *Green Eggs and Ham* and *Sneetches and Other Stories:* With his inimitable humor, vocabulary, and drawings this author writes about similarities and differences, and pokes fun at prejudice. New York, Random House, Inc. (Primary)

Slobodkin, Louis, *One Is Good, But Two Is Better:* A picture-story book with a cooperative theme. New York, The Vanguard Press. (Primary)

Sorensen, Virginia, *Plain Girl:* An Amish child is torn between family ties and the attraction of the world outside. New York, Harcourt, Brace & Company, Inc. (Upper Elementary)

Sterne, Emma Gelders, *Mary McLeod Bethune:* A well written biography of a great Negro educator. Spans the time from the Reconstruction period in American history to the present day. New York, Alfred A. Knopf, Inc. (Upper Elementary)

Tarry, Ellen, *My Dog Rinty:* A story with a background in Harlem, and the problem of how to make one's lively dog acceptable in a hostile neighborhood. New York, Viking Press, Inc. (Upper Elementary, but for all ages as well)

Taylor, Sidney, *All-of-a-Kind Family:* A Jewish family experiences the joys and sorrows of a close-knit family in New York's East Side at the turn of the century. New York, Follet Publishing Co. (Upper Elementary)

Thomas, Edith Lovell, *The Whole World Singing:* 99 songs from 40 countries, songs that have to do with work, play, and worship. New York, Friendship Press. (All ages)

Uchida, Yoshida, *New Friends for Susan:* A Japanese-American girl makes new friends when she goes to a different school. This is a sensitive picture of life in a Nisei family. New York, Charles Scribner's Sons. (Primary and older)

Uchida, Yoshida, *The Promised Year:* Keiko, a young Japanese girl, spends a year with her aunt and uncle in California. New York, Harcourt, Brace & Company, Inc. (Upper Elementary)

Weiss, Edna S., *Truly Elizabeth:* A ten-year-old Vermont farm girl upsets the residents of a New York City suburb in escapades with her new-found Negro friend, Ralph. Good pictures of a large city with its many races and religions. Boston, Houghton Mifflin, 1957.

White, Anne Terry, *George Washington Carver,* and *The American Indian:* Beautifully written and illustrated books with self-explanatory titles. New York, Random House, Inc. (All ages)

Wright, Betty Atwell, *Urban Picture Talks:* Series of albums, twelve or twenty-four large prints each using intergroup photographs and models as springboards for discussion and concept development. Concentrates on urban living and experiences. Teachers' guide. New York, The John Day Company, Inc. (All ages)

MORE BOOKS AND PAMPHLETS FOR OLDER STUDENTS
(Also see Adult list previously given)

Abrams, Charles, *Forbidden Neighbors:* Study of prejudice in housing. New York, Harper & Row Publishers, Inc.

Alpenfels, Ethel J., *Sense and Nonsense about Race:* Noted anthropologist presents facts to demolish race myths and superstitions. New York, Friendship Press.

Anderson, Marion, *My Lord, What a Morning:* Sensitive, warm autobiography of a great singer and her life. New York, The Viking Press.

Benedict, Ruth, *Patterns of Culture:* A long-time classic by a famous anthropologist. Cambridge, Harvard University Press.

Bond, Gladys Baker, *Little Stories on Big Subjects:* a box of seven short stories providing students with vicarious experiences in solving human relations problems. Anti-Defamation League.

Braithwaite, Edward Ricardo, *To Sir with Love:* The teacher was of a different race, but understanding came to a classroom of hostile teen-agers. New York, Prentice-Hall, Inc.

Brameld, Theodore, *The Remaking of a Culture: Life and Education in Puerto Rico.* New York, Harper and Brothers.

Buck, Pearl, *The Big Wave:* New York, The John Day Company, Inc.

Buck, Pearl, *The Good Earth:* New York, The John Day Company, Inc.

Buck, Pearl, *The Man Who Changed China:* New York, Random House, Inc.

Carruthers, Jeanne, *Fear Not:* A play about an Indian Christian professor who stops a student mob. One act. 9 characters. New York, Friendship Press.

Clayton, *Martin Luther King: The Peaceful Warrior.* New York, Prentice-Hall, Inc.

Cobb, Alice, *Come to Shanta Bhawan:* Story of American David Brown's visit to Nepal. Interweaves Himalayan adventure, Nepalese culture, and explorations of Hinduism, Judaism, and Christianity. New York, Friendship Press.

Colman, Hila, *The Girl from Puerto Rico:* The trials of a family newly arrived from Puerto Rico. New York, William Morrow and Company.

Courlander, Harold, *On Recognizing the Human Species:* A study showing that superficial social differences cannot disguise basic similarities of man's traditions, hopes, and customs the world over. Anti-Defamation League.

Covello, Leonard, *The Heart Is the Teacher.* New York, McGraw-Hill Book Company, Inc.

Daniels, Esther, *Paths That Cross:* A lively collection of stories, sketches, and clippings from African Journals. New York, Friendship Press.

Decter, Moshe, *A Fact-by-Fact Primer:* Analyzes Communist programs, strategies, and inconsistencies in question and answer form. New York, Collier Books.

Douglas, William O., *A Living Bill of Rights:* An explanation of why the Bill of Rights was and is necessary and how it protects individuals. Anti-Defamation League.

Drama Sampler: Handy resource of 28 plays for older students, as well as for adult and community use on intergroup education themes. New York, Friendship Press.

Epstein, Benjamin R., *Some of My Best Friends:* Penetrating study of anti-Semitism in education, employment, housing, and many aspects of American social life. New York, Farrar Straus and Cudahy.

Evans, Eva Knox, *All About Us:* Story of how people over the centuries changed in skin color, custom, and language. Easy reading and vocabulary. New York, Capitol Publishing Co., Inc.

Fisher, Lois J., *Bill and His Neighbors:* A young man's view of racial and religious prejudices and the problems they create in junior high school. Boston, Houghton Mifflin Company.

Frank, Anne, *Diary of a Young Girl:* This has become a classic, was made into a movie, and describes the horrifying and hopeless plight of a teen-age girl in a Nazi concentration camp. New York, Random House, Inc.

Griffin, John Howard, *Black Like Me:* Boston, Houghton Mifflin Company.

Handlin, Oscar, *American Jews: Their Story:* Anti-Defamation League.

Handlin, Oscar, *The Newcomers:* Cambridge, Harvard University Press.

Hanson, Earl Parker, *Puerto Rico: Land of Wonders:* New York, Alfred A. Knopf, Inc.

Hanson, Earl Parker, *Transformation: The Story of Modern Puerto Rico:* Simon & Schuster, Inc.

Harmon, Sidney, *Hand in Hand:* Based on the prize-winning motion picture, this story challenges interreligious barriers. New York, Whittlesey House.

Isaacs, Harold R., *The New World of Negro Americans:* New York, The John Day Company, Inc.

Julian, Joseph, *The Devil and The Dream:* A play. Anti-Defamation League.

Kelly, *Your Freedoms: The Bill of Rights:* New York, G. P. Putnam's Sons.

Kennedy, John F., *A Nation of Immigrants:* Bill of Rights explanation. Anti-Defamation League.

King, Martin Luther, *Why We Can't Wait:* New York, Harper & Row Publishers, Inc.

Lee, Alfred M., *Fraternities Without Brotherhood:* Boston, Beacon Press.

Lee, Alfred M., *How Do You Talk about People?* Anti-Defamation League.

Lerner, Marguerite Rush, *Red Man, White Man, African Chief,* Minneapolis, Medical Books.

Mead, Margaret, *Coming of Age in Samoa:* Gloucester, Peter Smith.

Mead, Margaret, *Cultural Patterns and Technical Change:* New York, New American Library of World Literature, Inc.

Mead, Margaret, *New Lives for Old:* New York, New American Library.

Montagu, Ashley, *Man: His First Million Years.*

Montagu, Ashley, *Man in Process*

Montagu, Ashley, *What We Know about Race,* Anti-Defamation League.

Pettigrew, Thomas F., *Epitaph for Jim Crow,* Anti-Defamation League.

Powdermaker, Hortense, *Probing Our Prejudices,* New York, Harper & Row Publishers, Inc.

Publications Office, Board of Education of City of New York
"The Negro in American History"
"Puerto Rican Profiles"

Raab, Earl, *Anatomy of Nazism,* Anti-Defamation League.

Roche, John P., *The Quest for the Dream,* Anti-Defamation League.

Rollins, *They Showed the Way:* New York, Crowell.

Roosevelt, Anna Eleanor, and Tor, Regina, "Growing Toward Peace," United Nations.

Schecter, *The Peaceable Revolution,* Boston, Houghton Mifflin Company.

Senior, Clarence, *Strangers—Then Neighbors,* Anti-Defamation League.

Sneider, Vern, *Teahouse of the August Moon:* New York, G. P. Putnam's Sons.

Steichen, Edward, *The Family of Man:* New York, Simon and Schuster, Inc.

Steward, Julian, *The People of Puerto Rico: A Study in Social Anthropology,* Urbana, University of Illinois Press.

Summer, William Graham, *Folkways:* New York, New American Library of World Literature, Inc.

Swan, Darius Leander, *Choral Drama:* Interpreting the world-wide struggle for justice. Flexible cast. New York, Friendship Press.

Van Til, William, *Prejudiced—How Do People Get That Way?* Anti-Defamation League.

Waltrip, Lela and Rufus, *Quiet Boy:* New York, Longmans, Green & Co.

West, Anne, *Heart-Sound of a Stranger.* A play of a Mexican woman and bigoted Americans. One act—7 characters. New York, Friendship Press.

Weil, Truda and Kohan, Frances H., "Men Are Brothers—Four Pageants." Anti-Defamation League.

THE NEGRO IN AMERICA

Although it has received scant attention in American schools and textbooks until recently, the story of the Negro in America is as long as the history of the country itself. It is a tragic story of oppression, failure, defeat and humiliation. But it is also an exciting story of amazing accomplishments in the face of fantastically overwhelming difficulties and of heroes and leaders of whom all Americans should be proud. It is a thoroughly American story, too, for the American Negro is a unique creation of American society, past and present, and he can have no future apart from it. Finally, it does not seem to be an exaggeration to say that the reverse of this last statement is also true; the future of America may well hinge on the future of the Negro American. Our position in the world at large, where power is more and more shifting to the nonwhite nations, is certainly affected by our race relations; and our most cherished values and ideals are being sorely tested by the Negro revolution.

The latter point is of course the crucial one. In moral and ethical terms there is no question about what is right and what is wrong in civil rights matters; nor is there any question about what

An annotated bibliography prepared by Sally Linett of the Scarsdale High School, Scarsdale, N.Y., during the summer of 1964 as part of the Board of Education School Improvement Fellowship Program for meritorious teachers.

must be done if we are to be true to our ideals. But the events of the past decade have shown how difficult it is to translate moral imperatives into practical realities. Indeed, each step forward seems to generate new conflict and confusion and we are only just beginning to realize how tremendous are the barriers of misunderstanding, unpreparedness, and fear which confront us.

Thus it is very appropriate that the schools are being called upon to take a more active role in the field of race relations. Not only are the schools at the very center of controversy in many areas while at the same time developing special programs to deal with the realities of desegregation, they are also looking for ways to increase understanding and encourage reflective thinking among students of all ages. In order to meet this responsibility many different approaches will be tried in every grade, but at the high school level a great increase in reading about all aspects of the problem is an obvious need. Fortunately, there is a rapidly growing source of material from which to choose. Some of it is described in this bibliography in the hope that teachers and students will be assisted in their search for books which are significant and stimulating.

While this is certainly not a complete review of books dealing with the Negro in America I have tried to examine a wide variety of texts which are generally available in public libraries and/or paperback editions. Books written in the last ten years have been emphasized since they throw more light on the contemporary situation, but the full span of Negro history is covered in several. There are some specialized studies, too, which deal with particular aspects of the Negro role in American history. In addition, there is a sampling of articles from popular periodicals and a list of additional resources for teachers. These resources, like many of the books, offer countless suggestions for further study.

SALLY LINETT
(Published with author's permission)

Allport, Gordon W., *The Nature of Prejudice*, Cambridge, Mass., Addison-Wesley Publishing Co., 1954. An exhaustive psychological analysis of the origins, forms and effects of group prejudice, hatred and conflict. Ways of overcoming prejudice are also analyzed. Dr. Allport includes the details of countless scientific studies in his text in a lively manner which holds the reader's interest. So much is covered, however, that it is necessary to read selectively. A valuable resource.

Ashmore, Harry S., *The Other Side of the Jordan*, N.Y., W. W. Norton and Co., 1960. A southern newspaperman, who won distinction for his opposition to Governor Faubus in the Little Rock crisis of 1957, examines the plight of Negroes outside the South. The book is an elaboration of a series of articles written for the N.Y. *Herald Tribune* and is thus easy reading. But it is also very forceful.

Ashmore describes the poverty, despair and determination of a variety of Harlem residents, including a porter, a politician, a labor leader and a leader of the Black Muslims. His chapter on Puerto Ricans in New York City, "The Uneasy Neighbors," is particularly interesting. Chapter 10, "The Uses of Law," is a valuable description of the activities of the N.Y. State Commission Against Discrimination, and there is also a brief description of an upper-middle-class Negro area in Mount Vernon.

Banfield, Edward C. and Wilson, James Q., "Negroes," *City Politics,* Cambridge, Mass., Harvard U. Press, 1963, pp. 293–312. A scholarly, detailed and yet very readable examination of the position of Negroes in city political life. Despite the fact that the number of Negroes in the larger cities has been increasing rapidly, relatively few Negroes are elected to public office. Nor do Negroes have the amount of influence in city government to which their numbers might seem to entitle them. Two interrelated factors account for this situation, according to the authors. One is the class structure of Negro society; the other is the character of urban political systems. The authors then offer a cogent review of much current information about Negro community life and an explanation of the ways in which Negroes participate in city politics.

Baldwin, James, *Nobody Knows My Name*, N.Y., Dell Paperback, 1954. A collection of essays, most dealing—directly or indirectly —with "the Negro problem." These essays require much from the reader, but most are worth the effort. Particularly good are those describing the effects of segregated schooling on Southern Negro children—"A Fly in the Buttermilk," and "Nobody Knows My Name." Less meaningful for the average reader are the last four essays, since they are analyses of four other artists—Gide, Bergmann, Wright, and Mailer. Much of the discussion revolves around

Baldwin's relationship to these men and full appreciation of his comments presupposes full acquaintance with their works.

"Fifth Avenue, Uptown," "East River, Downtown," and "Nobody Knows My Name" are similar to *The Fire Next Time*—but with much less bite and force. They may be valuable reading for help in understanding Baldwin's more outstanding work.

Baldwin, James, *The Fire Next Time,* N.Y., Dial Press, 1963. Mr. Baldwin's vigorous writing and controversial ideas have propelled him into national prominence as an intellectual leader of the Negro Revolution. Any attempt to understand race relations in the U.S. today should include a careful reading—and rereading—of this powerful book. A scathing yet compassionate critic of contemporary America, Baldwin aims to make his white readers understand the bitter anger of American Negroes and to accept their responsibility for it.

Bardolph, Richard, *The Negro Vanguard,* N.Y., Rinehart and Co., 1959. The history of Negroes in America is handled here in an interesting fashion. The author traces the achievements of Negro leaders during the last 200 years, thus studying "the history of the whole Negro American intellectual group, both in its own internal evolution and in its changing situation in the developing American social frame." This approach is much more inviting than that of the standard histories of the Negro and Bardolph's style is very pleasing. However, the tremendous number of individuals who are discussed and the resulting length of the book lessens its charm for the general reader. For selective studies of the effect of environment on Negroes in the U.S., or for background material for teaching American history from the point of view of heroes and leaders, this book should prove very valuable.

Boyle, Sarah Patton, *The Desegregated Heart,* N.Y., William Morrow and Co., 1962. This is an unusual book. Although it is a strong condemnation of Southern prejudice, it is not the usual "J'accuse" hurled by white (or Negro) liberals at the stubborn and misguided South. It is an explanation of Southern attitudes and traditions by a woman who learned them as part of her traditional aristocratic upbringing in Virginia. As such it should be enlightening for all who find the South puzzling or frightening—and for those who are quick to condemn the South in absolute terms.

The Desegregated Heart is also the moving story of one woman's attempt to break out of traditional patterns of thought and action in order to meet the challenge of desegregation, and of the spiritual anguish which she suffered. The last section of the book is a long and detailed account of Mrs. Boyle's religious faith.

Brink, William and Harris, Louis, *The Negro Revolution in America,*
    N.Y., Simon and Schuster, 1964. The editors of *Newsweek* and
    the well-known public-opinion pollster, Louis Harris, joined forces
    to probe the true attitudes of white and Negro Americans toward
    the social revolution which is now taking place in this country.
    The summary of their findings is combined with a brief but cogent
    history of Negroes in America and an analysis of the genesis of
    the Negro Revolt. The latter includes an examination of the im-
    portant role being played by the Negro churches. The confusions
    and contradictions in white attitudes toward Negroes is carefully
    documented, and the authors use the results of their research to
    describe what it is like to be a Negro in the U.S. This book has
    additional value as an introduction to the technique of public
    opinion polling.
Carmichael, Omer and Weldon, James, *The Louisville Story,* N.Y.,
    Simon and Schuster, 1957. A very optimistic tale of the successful
    desegregation of schools in a large southern city. Vigorous mod-
    erate leadership, careful planning and a firm commitment to law
    and order are given the major share of credit for Louisville's
    achievement. The authors also discuss problems with which the
    city officials had to contend and the various solutions which were
    used. A short book which is easy reading.
Clark, Kenneth B., *Prejudice and Your Child,* Boston, Beacon Press,
    1955. A distinguished social psychologist, whose studies on the
    effects of segregated schooling were cited in the Supreme Court's
    1954 desegregation decision, offers guidance to parents, teachers
    and school administrators. His goal: saving American children from
    the corrosive effects of prejudice. Although some of Dr. Clark's
    suggestions and predictions seem overly optimistic and even a bit
    naive, the book is nonetheless very valuable. His explanation of
    the origins of prejudice and its social and psychological effects is
    straightforward and convincingly illustrated. He incorporates into
    his text the results of much significant research without over-
    whelming the reader with statistics and complicated analysis. His
    excellent bibliography of material in learned journals would be
    very useful to anyone desiring to read the results of specialized
    studies in the psychology of prejudice and race relations.
Cook, James Graham, *The Segregationists,* N.Y., Appleton-Century-
    Crofts, 1962. Mr. Cook wishes to identify clearly the segregation-
    ists, those people who have so successfully prevented the imple-
    mentation of the Supreme Court's 1954 school decision. They are
    not, he says, just the cruel red-necks and misguided aristocrats who
    are so often described in the northern press. It is ". . . inaccurate,
    hazardously inaccurate, to think of the South's really influential

segregationists as cartoon figures . . . it tends to produce, I think, a meaningfully serious misunderstanding of the character of the South's resistance to racial integration and of the remarkable diversity of the men and women who are leading it."

In order to correct this misunderstanding the author visited and interviewed at length all of the important Southern segregationist leaders. Although they are a varied group who follow a range of occupations, most still emerge from these pages as cartoon characters in spite of Mr. Cook's efforts. They are convincingly portrayed but their ideas and attitudes are so extreme that they seem unreal. But the extent of their influence is made very real indeed, and "the reign of terror" which now exists in Mississippi and other parts of the South is chillingly portrayed.

Mr. Cook also makes a detailed examination of "Anti-Semitism Among the Magnolias," of which there is a great deal; and he reports on the effects of desegregation in Washington, D.C., from a very pessimistic point of view.

Cuban, Larry, ed., *The Negro in America,* Scott Foresman Problems in American History, Chicago, 1964. One of a series of source materials designed for use by American history students. A variety of materials—documents, letters, historical analyses, etc.—are organized around fifteen different aspects of the story of the Negro in America. Among these topics, or Problems as they are called, are "The Origin of Slavery," "Negroes and Reconstruction," "Class Structure in the Negro Community" and "New Patterns of Negro Leadership." Each problem is introduced by the editor in order to set it into historical perspective and to point out to the student the significant aspects of the readings which follow. Since contradictory analyses have been included at several points these suggestions, and accompanying study questions, should help the student to develop his critical abilities. Most of the selections are very good and many are excellent. Particularly interesting are several letters, journals, and excerpts from newspaper articles and out-of-print books—materials which are not readily available to student or teacher. The editor's introductions are well written.

An excellent volume which could be used in a variety of ways, some of which are suggested in the Editors' Introduction. It should be quite stimulating for the high school students for whom it was intended but might nonetheless be appropriate for advanced junior high school students, too.

Ellison, Ralph, *The Invisible Man,* N.Y., Random House, 1947. A fast-paced, gripping novel which is not always clear and is sometimes very disturbing. However, its hero is a vivid creation who is both an individual and, more important, a symbol of the tortured Negro in America. His experiences as a bright Negro boy who wishes to please the white leaders of his southern home town and the apparently obsequious president of the Negro college are particularly memorable for their sardonic revelations about the relationships between Negroes and whites. His later experiences in Harlem are more difficult to follow but illustrate a good deal of the squalor, confusion and disturbance of that community and how these factors are used by racist and conspiratorial groups. The story builds to the climax of the bloody race riot which may help readers understand the complexities of the 1964 disturbances in the Harlems of the North.

Ellison is often quoted because of his successful projection of a theme that runs through much contemporary Negro writing. This is the belief that the most difficult problem faced by the Negro is the refusal of the white world to see him as anything more than a symbol or a problem, the refusal, in short, to do the most fundamental thing—to see him as a man.

Elkins, Stanley M., *Slavery, A Problem in American Institutional and Intellectual Life,* University of Chicago Press, 1959. A brilliant expansion of Frank Tannenbaum's theory regarding the differences in the development of slavery in North and South America. Like Dr. Tennenbaum, Professor Elkins feels that the character of slavery in two areas was different because of the effect of other powerful institutions on the two societies. He supports Dr. Tennenbaum's belief that the Roman Catholic Church in Latin America, in cooperation with the authoritarian Spanish and Portuguese governments, controlled slavery in such a way that the slave remained a human being who could—and did—take his place as an equal in the larger society when his slave status was terminated. No comparable institutions existed in North America and the identification and treatment of the slave as less than human was the natural consequence.

Professor Elkins then goes on to ask the very significant question, "What effect did this treatment of the slave have upon his personality?" His startling answer: The Negro's personality was altered to an incredible degree. "Sambo" did exist on the southern plantation, Elkins feels, despite contemporary efforts to dismiss the term as a meaningless stereotype. But the Sambo personality was not the result of inherent racial inferiority nor the product of a primitive African culture as is so often charged. The utterly dependent and childlike Negro was the product of the peculiar system of slavery as it developed in the U.S., a system of absolute power. Professor Elkins explains, expands and supports his theory using mainly two kinds of material. One is drawn from the theoretical knowledge presently available in social psychology, and the other is derived from data that have come out of German concentration camps. Prof. Elkins' theory is both startling and controversial, but it opens possibilities for understanding some of the critical psychological aspects of the relations of Negroes to American society. Some of them are explored by Charles Silberman in *Crisis in Black and White.* Professor Elkins' book requires, and deserves, careful study.

Franklin, John Hope, *From Slavery to Freedom,* Second Edition, N.Y. Knopf, 1956. A complete and comprehensive general history of Negroes in the western hemisphere. The book begins with a review of the great mingling of races in ancient Egypt and a history of Negro civilizations in Africa. All aspects of the slave trade in North and South America are examined as are the details of "that peculiar institution" as it developed in all parts of this hemisphere. The Civil War is thoroughly analyzed and nearly 400 pages are devoted to the history of America's Negro citizens during the last 100 years. A superior resource for teacher and student, this book is excellent for both research and general reading. An exhaustive bibliography is included.

Frazier, E. Franklin, *Black Bourgeoisie,* Glencoe, Illinois, 1957, Collier Books Paperback, 1962. A harsh picture of the Negro middle class by one of the foremost authorities on Negro family life. Prof. Frazier feels that the minority of Negroes who are relatively well off (those who have incomes above $4,000 per year) live in a world of fantasy which is in large measure created, and fed, by the Negro press. All of the worst aspects of the white society—its trappings and status symbols—are emulated and worshiped; but little real effort is made to compete or copy the Whites in terms of substance or achievement.

Professor Frazier also offers a critical analysis of the philosophy, curricula, problems and achievements of Negro colleges. His style is pleasing and the book is easy reading. The 1962 paperback edition contains a new preface by the author.

Frazier, E. Franklin, *The Negro in the United States,* N.Y., Macmillan, 1957 (rev. ed.). The late head of the Department of Sociology at Howard University wrote an exhaustive history of American Negroes from the sociologist's point of view. Thus the emphasis is on institutions—churches, the family, schools, fraternal organizations, etc.—and the processes by which Negroes have developed their own community in relation to the larger American community. Useful for selective reading or as a research tool, this excellent book contains a wealth of detail and is very well written.

212   EDUCATING FOR DIVERSITY

Glazer, Nathan and Moynihan, Daniel, *Beyond the Melting Pot,* Cam-
     bridge, Mass., Harvard University Press, 1963. The basic premise
     of this book is that the melting pot did not happen. "The notion
     that the intense and unprecedented mixture of ethnic and religious
     groups in American life was soon to blend into a homogeneous
     end product has outlived its usefulness and credibility." To explain
     this thesis the authors examine five major ethnic groups in New
     York City which, they point out, may not be all or even most of
     America, but "surely is the most important single part." They feel
     that religion and race will define the next stage in the evolution of
     the American peoples and it is thus essential to understand the
     real roles of various ethnic groups as they exist today.
        The first two groups which they depict are the Negroes and the
     Puerto Ricans. Although the average white observer may tend to
     lump Negroes and Puerto Ricans together there are distinct dif-
     ferences in history, culture, psychology and economic situation
     between the two groups. There are thus significant differences in
     their position in New York today. The authors' examination of
     New York's Negro community is all-inclusive and covers several
     topics which are not often discussed with such candor. For ex-
     ample, they explain why genuinely integrated housing in the cities
     and suburbs is a very elusive goal, and describe the growing ten-
     sions between Negroes and Jews in New York City. The authors
     conclude this section of their book with the suggestion that the
     present Negro leadership in New York is mistaken in its emphasis
     on protest. Instead they urge greater emphasis on self-help, that
     is on Negro efforts to solve Negro problems.
        This willingness to discuss aspects of New York City life which
     are rarely mentioned in print lends excitement to Glazer and
     Moynihan's work. They display additional virtues. They are thor-
     ough without being tedious and scholarly without being dull.
     Chapters 1, 2, and 6 and the authors' introduction are essential
     reading for anyone seeking an up-to-date picture of race relations
     in New York City; however, the entire book is recommended for
     its unusual but significant approach to American history. The ex-
     tensive footnotes suggest many possibilities for further reading.
Greenberg, Jack, *Race Relations and American Law,* N.Y., Columbia
     University Press, 1959. A scholarly and encyclopedic examination
     of all aspects of the laws dealing with race relations in the United
     States. The first chapter is an analysis, from both the philosophic
     and technical points of view, of the capacity of law to alter race
     relations. Can laws create or end discrimination and prejudice?
     Or must change await developments in the hearts and minds of
     men? Although this chapter, like the rest of the book, would be

fully appreciated only by lawyers and sociologists, any mature and careful reader should find it rewarding. The chief value of the book for high school students would be as a reference work. It also contains an excellent bibliography of material published before 1959. Mr. Greenberg is Chief Counsel for the NAACP Legal Defense Fund, the organization which has assumed the responsibility for almost all of the important civil rights cases.

Greene, Lorenzo, *The Negro in Colonial New England, 1620–1776,* N.Y., Columbia University Press, 1942. A fascinating examination of a little-known aspect of American history. Slavery was common in colonial New England and many New England fortunes—including that of the family for which Brown University is named— were based on the slave trade. The author discusses all aspects of the Negro's life in New England, his occupations, his position before the law, his family life, etc., quoting liberally from a great variety of original sources. There were important differences between slavery in New England and in the southern colonies and Mr. Greene discusses these briefly.

A few of the chapters are marred for the general reader by an excessive number of facts and footnotes, but the book should nevertheless prove rewarding for anyone interested in a detailed study of one period of the history of the Negro in America.

Griffin, John Howard, *Black Like Me,* Boston, Houghton Mifflin Co., 1960. An amazing story which demonstrates with shocking clarity the constant humiliation which is inflicted on the Negro in the South. With the help of medicine and cosmetics the author lived as a Negro in Mississippi, Louisiana and other southern states. His book "traces the changes that occur to heart and body and intelligence when a so-called first-class citizen is cast on the junkheap of secondary class citizenship." It is also a crude and yet compassionate picture of the self-destruction of southern whites.

Mr. Griffin's uncomplicated style and the book's underlying tone of sadness add to the force of his story. A very effective introduction to the realities of segregation. Easy reading.

Handlin, Oscar, *Race and Nationality in American Life,* Boston, Little, Brown and Co., 1957. The origins of prejudice against ethnic groups and non-whites are traced and explained. Particularly interesting is Professor Handlin's description of the development of the idea of "good" and "bad" immigrants and the "scientific" thinking which was used to support the idea of superior and inferior racial and ethnic stocks. Such ideas were very popular in the 1920s and 1930s and were supported by many respectable scientists of that time, Prof. Handlin shows. There is an interesting

and over-long discussion of the connection between 19th century
sexual standards and ethnic prejudice.

Handlin, Oscar, *The Uprooted,* Boston, Little, Brown and Co., 1951.
The southern Negro who migrates to the big cities of the North
experiences many of the same difficulties which beset the many
other migrants who preceded him. Thus an understanding of the
history of the American Negro requires an understanding of "the
epic story of the great migrations that made the American people."
In this prize-winning book, Prof. Handlin describes in vivid detail
the hardships and achievements of each of the ethnic groups which
came to America. He believes that the relationship between the
immigrants and America was significant for both. The immigrants
were of course influenced by American mores and institutions, but
they in turn made profound impact on America. They have shaped
mores and institutions and the process is not a completed one.

Handlin, Oscar, *The Newcomers,* Cambridge, Mass., Harvard University Press, 1959. Prof. Handlin continues his study of ethnic minorities with this volume on Negro and Puerto Rican migration to
New York City. He explains the position of these two groups as
another chapter in the continuing story of immigrant minorities
in America. Thus he believes that their problems, great as they
are, are essentially the same as those of earlier migrants and will
be solved in the same fashion. (This "acculturation thesis" is
criticized by Charles Silberman in *Crisis in Black and White* and
is rejected by other writers including James Baldwin and Rev.
Martin Luther King.) Although they are pedantic in tone Professor Handlin's books nonetheless make very lively reading.

Harrington, Michael, *The Other America,* N.Y., Macmillan, 1963;
Penguin Paperback, 1964. The racial problem is inextricably inter-
twined with America's other major social difficulty—the problem
of poverty. In *The Other America* Michael Harrington tries to
make us aware of the 40 to 50 million people who "constitute a
subculture of poverty" virtually out of the sight of the rest of
America. They include the migrant farm workers, the unskilled,
the aged and the one quarter of the inhabitants of the other
America who are Negro. Negroes thus suffer a double disability,
for, as Mr. Harrington points out, even if all discrimination is
wiped out their problems will still be a long, long way from solution. He points out, for example, that in a recent year, Negro unemployment in New York City was somewhat more than double
that of the whites and their wages were around one-half of what
white workers got. The author uses such statistics throughout his
book to substantiate his conclusions, but they never get in the way
of his fast-paced and very interesting narrative.

Chapter 4, "If You're Black, Stay Back," is specifically concerned with the Negro residents of the other America, but the entire book should be read by all social studies students.

Isaacs, Harold R., *The New World of Negro Americans*, N.Y., The John Day Company, Inc., 1963. Mr. Isaacs seeks "to show how the end of white supremacy in the world is forcing the end of the white supremacy system in the U.S." In doing so he discusses the question of color as it relates to the rapid emergence of new nations in Africa and Asia and the effect of this situation on U.S. foreign and domestic policy; the connection between nineteenth century colonialism and racism in the U.S.; the terribly difficult problem of identity which is faced by Negro Americans and the easing of this problem which the emergence of African nations has caused. His book is in part an extended treatment of the themes of James Baldwin, Charles Silberman, Richard Wright, and the many other writers who have been concerned with the problem of Negro identity. His discussion of the psychological effect on Negro children of decades of public school teaching about Africa as a land of savages and cannibals is particularly absorbing. So is his description of the surprising difficulties encountered by Negro Americans who seek to "return" to Africa. He also devotes considerable attention to six Negro writers, W. E. B. DuBois, Langston Hughes, Richard Wright, Ralph Ellison, James Baldwin, and Lorraine Hansbury.

Although it is written from the point of view of the academic social scientist this book is thoroughly absorbing. Prof. Isaacs writes in an informal manner, incorporating excerpts from extended interviews with 107 Negroes, most of them individuals of considerable achievement. He concludes by raising some difficult questions which will face American Negroes as integration becomes more of a reality.

There is an excellent bibliography which includes many references to Negro publications and to sociological and psychiatric journals.

Javits, Jacob K., *Discrimination, U.S.A.*, N.Y., Harcourt, Brace & Co., 1960. The senior Senator from New York is optimistic about the long-range improvement of race relations in the U.S. He describes difficulties faced by minorities in the past and the great strides towards equality which have been taken by many. He also describes the problems in employment, education, housing, politics, etc. faced by Negroes today and the efforts which are being made to overcome them. Senator Javits is convinced that laws passed and enforced by responsible governments can be a tremendously effective instrument of social progress. He describes the effect of laws which have been passed by many states and cities in order to support his thesis, and also explains the tremendous changes which have taken place in Washington, D.C. since an official policy of desegregation was adopted there.

The wealth of facts and figures about particular problems of discrimination make this book valuable as a research tool. It is also very readable.

Kilpatrick, James Jackson, *The Southern Case for School Segregation*, N.Y., Crowell-Collier, 1962. A recent book by a southern newspaper editor which calmly presents the reasons for southern resistance to desegregation. The warm relationships between Virginia whites and Negroes is described in terms of the author's personal experiences. He also explains the difficulties which Southerners foresee if integration is forced upon the South. The bibliography is very interesting, because Mr. Kilpatrick describes many pro-integration books from a southern point of view.

Kilpatrick, James Jackson, *The Sovereign States, Notes of a Citizen of Virginia*, Chicago, Regnery, 1957. J. W. Peltason in his bibliographical notes for *58 Lonely Men* refers to this book as "the most scholarly" of the few books written by avowed segregationists. In it Kilpatrick, who is editor of the Richmond, Virginia, *New Leader*, defends states' rights and white supremacy.

King, Martin Luther, Jr., *Stride Toward Freedom*, The Montgomery Story, N.Y., Harper & Bros., 1958. The man who is often referred to as the principal leader of the Negro Revolution tells the story of the event which propelled him into national and international prominence. The day-to-day evolution of the bus strike in Montgomery is told with a good deal of dramatic impact, but the book is more important for its exposition of the philosophy of nonviolence. Reverend King explains himself, his philosophy, and the crusade which he heads with humility and simplicity.

King, Martin Luther, Jr., *Why We Can't Wait*, N.Y., Harper & Row, and New American Library (paper), 1964. Rev. King recounts the history of the civil rights movement and explains its goals in a manner which caused the *New York Times* reviewer to comment: "No clearer statement of the present mood of the colored people has come to this reviewer's attention."

Lincoln, C. Eric, *The Black Muslims*, Boston, Beacon Press, 1961. White racism has spawned several different groups dedicated to black racism. The latest and most ominous is the group known as the Black Muslims. Dr. Lincoln describes the group's origins, beliefs and achievements (which are considerable), and explains why it may increase in size and potential danger.

Linton, Ralph, *The Tree of Culture,* N.Y., 1955, Alfred A. Knopf, Inc. This outstanding work of cultural anthropology contains a chapter on "African Civilization." Dr. Linton feels that "few Americans realize how rich and complex the cultures of many African societies were at the time of the first European contact." His analysis of the history of the regions from which the ancestors of American Negroes were drawn disproves the myth that Negroes have contributed nothing to civilization.

Lomax, Louis, *The Negro Revolt,* N.Y., Harper & Row, 1962; Reprint: Signet Books, 1963. A very good summary of the history of Negroes in America, including an analysis of why Negroes were unable to fully develop a separate culture. *The Negro Revolt* is particularly valuable for its explanation of the emergence of new Negro leadership in the last ten years, and the important growth of mass participation—particularly by young people—in the struggle for full Negro equality. Lomax also analyzes the various Negro organizations and leaders, all of whom he knows personally, and explains their relationships to the Negro and white communities. Although some of the material in the last few chapters is a bit dated, even these chapters are valuable reading, especially for the author's analysis of President Kennedy's attitude toward civil rights and the connection between the world racial problem and that of the U.S.

Lomax, Louis, *The Reluctant African,* N.Y., Harper and Bros., 1960. Because events in Africa move so fast that "men and situations alter before anything written about them can possibly get into print," much of this book is dated. However, it is still important because of the author's success in illuminating the explosive quality of anti-white feeling in Africa. As a Negro reporter he had experiences and opportunities a white man could not have. He visited the home of one of Tom Mboya's aides in an "African dwelling," a primitive government housing project on the outskirts of Nairobi, for example, and later was taken to a night-long tribal rally in the Kenya Highlands. He also met with underground leaders in South Africa after outwitting the governmental authorities in proper cloak and dagger style. He demonstrates the striking parallel between anti-white racism in Africa and anti-black racism in the U.S., and shows how the Chinese, the Egyptians and the Russians are all taking advantage of this situation.

Mr. Lomax writes a subjective report with considerable dramatic flair. His book is useful material for developing an understanding of the origins and dangers of racism. It would be valuable also as supplementary reading in the study of colonialism or the problems of the emerging nations.

Muse, Benjamin, *Ten Years of Prelude,* N.Y., Viking Press, 1964.
A journalist with a background in politics (he was formerly a
Virginia State Senator), Mr. Muse made a three year study of the
southern reaction to the historic school desegregation decision.
The result is a very complete record of the developments of the
past ten years. It is an excellent source for anyone wishing to know
the full story of events in such places as Little Rock, Clinton, Tennessee, Oxford, Mississippi, etc. There is also a great deal of information about communities which successfully avoided racial
strife.

Mr. Muse sees a promising pattern in the events of the last ten
years and feels that the extreme segregationists have, by and
large, finally been overcome. His last chapter is an interesting
analysis of the long-range significance of "The Revolution." The
text of the Supreme Court decision in Brown v. Topeka is in the
Appendix.

Myrdal, Gunnar, *An American Dilemma: The Negro Problem and
Modern Democracy,* N.Y., Harper and Bros., 1944. Probably the
most quoted and most respected single work on the Negro in
America, Dr. Myrdal's study is usually described as "monu-
mental." The adjective applies both to its size (over 1,000 pages
in 2 volumes) and to its importance. With the help of many noted
scholars, including Ralph Bunche, Dr. Myrdal chronicled every
aspect of the relationship between whites and Negroes in the
U.S. Dr. Myrdal's basic thesis—that white Americans are torn
between their belief in the American creed and its conflict with
their behavior towards Negroes—is now seriously questioned by
many observers. (See, e.g., Gordon Allport, *The Nature of Prejudice,* p. 329 and Charles Silberman, *Crisis in Black and White,*
p. 10.) But his exhaustive study is still the guidepost for all that
have come after. A condensed version is in paperback: Arnold
Rose, *The Negro in America,* N.Y., Harper Torchbooks, 1964.

Oliver, Roland and Fage, J. D., *A Short History of Africa,* N.Y., N.Y.
University Press, 1963. A brief but apparently complete history of
Africa from prehistoric times to the present Congo crisis. The
wealth of detail which is included makes this book too difficult for
general reading. But it is a valuable research tool.

Peltason, Jack W., *58 Lonely Men,* N.Y., Harcourt, Brace & World,
1961. "The Constitution may be what the Supreme Court says it
is, but a Supreme Court opinion means, for the moment at least,
what the district judge says it means." Prof. Peltason tells the
behind-the-headlines story of the 58 federal district and circuit
judges in the South whose responsibility it is to carry out the
Supreme Court decision outlawing segregation. In doing so he

presents a very detailed, though smoothly written, discussion of many cases related to the Brown decisions—for example, cases concerning desegregation of particular school districts and cases arising out of state laws aimed at crippling the NAACP. He also explains why the Supreme Court's decision upholding the pupil placement laws of the southern states "must be chalked up as the most important prosegregation legal victory since Plessy v. Ferguson."

Professor Peltason shows how federal judges in the South have permitted and even encouraged the great variety of delaying tactics of southern school boards. But he also points out that "whatever desegregation there has been has come about because a judge has insisted on it." The author believes that such positive judicial action must receive active support and encouragement from top state and national political figures and describes the devastating effect of the lack of such leadership in Clinton, Tenn., Little Rock, Ark., and Prince Edward County, Va. His accounts of these and other violent episodes is a well-documented and absorbing description of this very disturbing aspect of recent American history.

The author's bibliographical notes are excellent. He includes a list of significant articles from law reviews and other legal and political journals.

Proudfoot, Merrill, *Diary of a Sit-in*, N.Y., Van Rees Press, 1962. The day-by-day diary which was kept by a white minister who was a leader of a sit-in movement in Knoxville, Tenn. Rev. Proudfoot's style is straightforward, quietly dramatic and absorbing. He illuminates the complex motivations, actions, and reactions of people on both sides of the controversy, thus giving the sit-in movement considerably more reality than it had in newspaper reports. His diary is very interesting, too, because of the insight it gives into the question of individual commitment—its challenges, costs and rewards.

Rose, Arnold, *The Negro in America*, N.Y., Harper Torchbooks, 1964. A one volume condensation of Gunnar Myrdal's *An American Dilemma*. See summary above.

Rowan, Carl T., *Go South to Sorrow*, N.Y., Random House, 1957. Carl T. Rowan, who was made chairman of the U.S. Information Agency by President Johnson in 1964, wrote this book while he was working for the Minneapolis *Tribune*. It is an impassioned recital of the events in the South during the mid-1950s. Mr. Rowan describes in great detail the activities of the White Citizens Council and many similar groups which were born during that period. The death in Mississippi of Emmet Till, a Negro boy from Chicago, and the world-wide criticism of the acquittal of his murderers, the harrowing experiences of Autherine Lucy when she integrated the University of Alabama, and the day by day progress of the famous Montgomery bus boycott are among the many disturbing events which he describes. He bemoans the lack of responsible white leadership in the South and shows how the few people of courage who did speak out in favor of law and order were systematically and effectively intimidated by the segregationists.

The author's continuous editorializing weakens his effectiveness and makes his book a bit dull in spots. However, he does have a flair for dramatic detail and many of his tales are told with you-are-there effectiveness. His book is generally useful for reviewing or learning about the situation in the South in the years following the Supreme Court's historic school desegregation decision. In addition, his description of attitudes and events in Mississippi is valuable background material for anyone trying to understand the situation in that state during the summer of 1964.

Silberman, Charles, *Crisis in Black and White*, N.Y., Random House, 1964. "What we are discovering, in short, is that the United States —all of it, North as well as South, West as well as East—is a racist society in a sense and to a degree that we have refused so far to admit, much less face." "The Negro will be unable to take his place in the main stream of American life until he stops despising himself and his fellows." There are two examples of the blunt language in this hard-hitting, thorough analysis of America's racial crisis. Silberman deals with all aspects of the problem, summarizing the history of the Negro in America from the period of the slave trade through the 1963 church bombing in Birmingham. He criticizes the stereotyped thinking of many integrationists and points out that Negroes are not just white men with black skins whose problems will be over once the white world learns the secret of brotherhood. He also assesses white responsibility for the present crisis. He explains the cumulative effect on Negro personality and behavior of 350 years of white oppression, rejection and manipulation. He demolishes two of the most popular arguments against immediate action, a) that Negroes must change before whites abandon discrimination; and b) that it is impossible to legislate morality.

Crisis in Black and White is both a summary of most of the significant facts and ideas about "the Negro problem" and a creative presentation of new ways of attacking it. A most important and exciting book. It should be widely read.

Tannenbaum, *Slave and Citizen, The Negro in the Americas*, N.Y., Knopf, 1947. The author contrasts the history of slavery in Spanish and Portuguese America with that of the slave system in the

Anglo-Saxon and French dominated areas. His purpose is to explain the violence which accompanied the abolition of slavery in the U.S. and the American Negro's subsequent failure to achieve acceptance as a full and equal member of the society. Professor Tannenbaum demonstrates that the feudal tradition in Latin American countries in conjunction with the strong position of the Roman Catholic Church in those areas endowed the slave with a legal and moral position which made gradual freedom for slaves both proper and possible. Paradoxically, it was the absence of these authoritarian influences in the American countries of Anglo-Saxon heritage which led to a slave system from which no gradual escape was possible for either Negroes or whites. Because the Common Law and Anglo-Saxon tradition made no provision for slavery, Professor Tannenbaum feels, it was necessary to develop ways of handling the institution and a philosophy to explain it. How could this be done by a society which proclaimed the equality of human beings? Only by concluding that the Negro was inherently inferior and treating him as chattel. Thus it was quite possible for the same people who wrote the Declaration of Independence to treat black Americans with incredible cruelty both before and after the issuance of the Emancipation Proclamation.

This small book is invaluable not only for the elaboration of this fascinating thesis, but also because of the author's detailed description of the slave trade, the relationship of master and slave in both North and South America, etc. He also incorporates many illuminating quotations from original sources into his text. It would be excellent supplementary reading for American history, Latin American studies, or even the study of feudalism and the Roman Catholic Church in World history.

Wilson, James, *Negro Politics,* Glencoe, Illinois, The Free Press, 1960. A very detailed and complicated analysis of Negro leadership in Chicago, Illinois. There are also some comparisons with New York, Philadelphia, Detroit and Los Angeles. Although Mr. Wilson's book is too difficult for general reading, selected chapters would be valuable as introductions to concentrated and "in-depth" sociological analysis. Among the best are Chapter V, "The Context of Negro Civic Life in the North," Chapter VI, "Negro Civic Forces in Chicago," Chapter VIII, "Negro-White Civic Relations," and Chapter IX, "Political Styles."

Woodward, C. Vann, *The Strange Career of Jim Crow,* N.Y., Oxford University Press, 1955. A short but fascinating analysis of the creation of the legal basis for segregation. Prof. Woodward demonstrates that Jim Crow laws, racial strife and the segregation of the Negro were not natural and inevitable developments in the South. Indeed, he shows that there were forces which held racism in check in the South until the 1890s and that a great degree of acceptance of the Negro existed for about thirteen years after the end of Reconstruction. The about-face which took place in the last decade of the 19th century is explained by Prof. Woodward as part of his effort to show that segregation and Negro disenfranchisement are not immutable and unchangeable aspects of southern folkways. He is therefore quite optimistic about the prospects for great improvements in racial relations and cites many developments of the forties and fifties which he feels support his optimism. Prof. Woodward's discussion of the development of the Populist movement in the South is very interesting. There is a short but useful bibliography.

Wright, Richard, *Black Boy*, N.Y., Harper and Bros., 1937. "Well-intentioned whites are surprised by the depth of Negro anger and frequently talk as if it were something new; they read James Baldwin with a shock of discovery, not knowing that Richard Wright was saying the same things twenty-five and thirty years ago." (Silberman, *Crisis in Black and White*, p. 58.)

Like Baldwin, Wright wants to show what white-instigated degradation has done to the Negro, and the price whites are paying for their "superiority." He is particularly effective in *Black Boy*, the story of his childhood in Jackson, Mississippi.

Ziegler, Benjamin M., ed., *Desegregation and the Supreme Court*. Problems in American Civilization Series, Boston, D. C. Heath & Co., 1958. Like the other books in this excellent series, this is a group of readings selected by the Department of American Studies at Amherst College. Its focus is the 1954 desegregation decision, Brown v. Topeka, and the tremendous power of the Supreme Court in the development of such historic issues. There are essays on the 1954 case and on the role of the Supreme Court as well as excerpts from eight major Supreme Court decisions. These decisions illustrate both the evolution of the doctrine of judicial review and the changing attitudes of the court toward the Negro and civil rights. Part III demonstrates the strong negative reaction which the Brown decision evoked. The attacks are directed both at the decision itself and at the right of the court to make such important decisions. A valuable source of supplementary reading for American studies and American history.

ARTICLES in PERIODICAL LITERATURE

Alsop, Stewart and Quayle, Oliver, "What Northerners Really Think of Negroes," *Saturday Evening Post*, Sept. 7, 1963, p. 17. Widespread interviews conducted by a journalist and a public opinion pollster revealed a tremendous amount of prejudice against Negroes in the North and West as well as the South. The comments of many of those interviewed are quoted at length and the authors conclude that there will be a great deal of resistance to genuine integration throughout the country.

Dugger, Ronnie, "These Are The Times: On Being a Southern Liberal," *Commentary,* April, 1964, p. 40. The moving personal story of a Texas editor who has attempted to live by his democratic convictions in a most hostile enviroment, East Texas.

Dykeman, Wilma and Stokely, James, "New Southerner: The Middle-Class Negro," *N.Y. Times Magazine,* August 9, 1959, p. 11. The authors describe the rapid growth of a Negro middle class in the South, especially in Atlanta, and discuss its possible effects on race relations.

Fischer, John, "What the Negro Needs Most: A First Class Citizens Council," *Harper's,* February, 1962, p. 12. The Editor of *Harper's* urges Negroes to work hard to eliminate the causes of white prejudice against them. He suggests that Negroes must earn the right to the equality which they desire. Although he admits that most of the antisocial behavior of Negroes has its origin in the oppressive tactics of American whites he feels that the Negroes must make a determined effort to improve themselves. He cites the high rate of crime and delinquency among Negroes, their generally poor record in school (as compared with whites) and other statistics which he feels make it unrealistic to expect even the best intentioned whites to accept integration. Such statements were bound to be controversial and the many Letters to the Editor in the September, 1962 and October, 1962 issues of *Harper's* reflect a wide variety of reactions.

Gibel, Inde Lederer, "How *Not* to Integrate the Schools," *Harper's,* November, 1963, pp. 57–66. The white mother of two Negro children urges northern civil rights leaders to reconsider their goals. Continued insistence on the complete integration of schools in New York and other northern cities will not solve the Negroes' problems and may even "destroy the very goals we seek." Mrs. Gibel feels that the problem of the northern Negro is more a problem of class and economics than a problem of color. She criticizes the unrealistic attitudes of many of the leaders (and followers) in the civil rights movement and makes many suggestions for realistic solutions of immediate problems. A well-written and provocative article.

Hacker, Andrew, "What Kind of a Nation Are We?" *N.Y. Times Magazine,* December 8, 1963, p. 23. As part of an analysis of contemporary America Professor Hacker explains why he believes that reaching a solution of our racial problems will be much more difficult than most national leaders have been willing to admit.

Hammer, Richard, "Report From a Spanish Harlem Fortress," *N.Y. Times Magazine,* January 5, 1964, p. 22. The author records his conversation with a teen-age resident of one of the worst parts of Spanish Harlem. The description of slum life and attitudes is graphic and clearly indicates the great lack of communication between "the other America" and the affluent majority.

Handlin, Oscar, "Is Integration the Answer?" *Atlantic,* April, 1964, p. 49. One of the foremost authorities on the role of minorities in American history examines the special situation of American Negroes, most particularly the changes of the last few years. He urges Negroes to clarify their goals and to see that integration in the North is only a means toward equality. His explanation of the need for clarification is itself not too clear, but the article as a whole is thought provoking.

Leonard, George, "A Southerner Appeals to the North: Don't Make Our Mistake," *Look,* August 11, 1964, p. 15. The Senior Editor of *Look,* a white man who was born and bred in a small Georgia town, describes Southern segregationists as mentally ill and urges the nation's leaders to force integration quickly in order to save the nation from disaster. A powerful essay which echoes, from the white point of view, James Baldwin's *The Fire Next Time.*

"Liberalism and the Negro, A Round-Table Discussion," *Commentary,* March, 1964, pp. 25–42. The edited transcript of a three hour discussion between James Baldwin, Nathan Glazer, Sidney Hook, and Gunnar Myrdal. The main topics under discussion were Mr. Baldwin's alleged claim that all whites are guilty of crimes against Negroes and that white liberals are perhaps the most guilty of all.

Long, M., "A Southern Teenager Speaks His Mind," *N.Y. Times Magazine,* November 10, 1963, p. 15. The thought processes and attitudes of an attractive young man from an old, substantial Mississippi family are clearly presented, mostly in his own words.

Miller, William Lee, "Analysis of the White Backlash," *N.Y. Times Magazine,* August 23, 1964, p. 27. A very helpful explanation of the reaction against the civil rights movement by many decent white Americans.

Morgan, Charles, "I Saw a City Die," *Look,* December 3, 1963, p. 23. Charles Morgan was a lawyer in Birmingham, Alabama, during the racial disturbances which included the bombing of Negro Sunday school students. One of the few whites who spoke out against the city administration, Mr. Morgan felt that the white moderates who "didn't want to get involved" and the business leaders who would not speak out were guilty of turning the city over to the forces of disorder. He describes the entire situation with a great deal of personal feeling.

Pike, Rt. Rev. James A., "The Roots of Bias," *Look,* March 14, 1961, pp. 49–52. The Bishop of the Episcopal Diocese of California discusses the commissions and omissions of churches in intergroup relations. Although his principal concern is the perpetuation of religious prejudice, Rev. Pike also discusses ways in which churches contribute to the continuation of racial prejudice.

Podhoretz, Norman, "My Negro Problem—And Ours," *Commentary,* February, 1963, p. 93. A searingly frank article in which the Editor of *Commentary* examines his feelings (and the feelings of white liberals in general) toward Negroes and concludes that the problem of inter-racial relations is a great deal more difficult than anyone is willing to admit. He feels that the only real solution to the problem will be the complete physical integration of the two races, since the kind of hatred which exists is too deeply rooted in society to be exorcised by any less powerful remedy.

Mr. Podhoretz's confessions caused a great deal of comment, some favorable, some critical, but all of it very interesting. For example, see *Commentary,* April, 1963, p. 338; *New Republic,* March 23, 1963, p. 11; and Silberman, *Crisis in Black and White,* p. 185.

Samuels, Gertrude, "Feud Within the Black Muslims," *N.Y. Times Magazine,* March 22, 1964, p. 17. An explanation of the Negro movement for black supremacy which emphasizes the differences among the group's leaders over programs and policy.

Taper, B., "Reporter at Large," *New Yorker,* June 10, 1961, p. 37 and June 17, 1961, p. 39. A detailed but very gripping story of the attempts of Negroes to register to vote in Tuskegee, Alabama.

Thompson, Robert Farris, "African Dancers at the Fair," *Saturday Review,* July 25, 1964, p. 37. A short explanation of African dancing which repudiates "Uncle Tom-Tomism, or the bigoted assumption that African culture is intrinsically sexy, savage and and sinister." When Americans watch Africans dance, Thompson feels, they are blinded by their assumption that the Africans are primitive savages. Thus they don't see the subtlety, intricacy and wit of "one of the most remarkable art forms on earth."

Toynbee, Arnold, "Is a Racial War in the Making?" *N.Y. Times Magazine,* September 29, 1963, p. 14. The renowned historian discusses the international implications of racial tension and hostility.

Walker, Gerald, "How Women Won the Quiet Battle of Atlanta," *Good Housekeeping,* May, 1962, p. 77. An encouraging story of effective civic action in Atlanta. The public schools in that southern city

were integrated peacefully in 1961 because of the careful work of a
group of housewives, most of whom had never been involved in
public affairs before. This article chronicles their successful struggle against segregationists (in and out of public office), apathy
and fear.

Young, Whitney M., Jr., "The Role of the Middle Class Negro,"
Ebony, September, 1963, p. 67. Mr. Young, the head of the Urban
League, is concerned about the cleavage which he sees between the
Negro middle class and the very large group of Negroes who are
in the very low income group.

ADDITIONAL RESOURCES

Brooks, Alexander D., *Civil Rights and Liberties in the U.S.: An Annotated Bibliography,* Civil Liberties Educational Foundation, 200
Park Ave., South, N.Y., 1961. Under the auspices of the Civil
Liberties Educational Foundation and with the assistance of teachers in the New York City schools, Prof. Brooks of Rutgers Law
School prepared a 151-page annotated bibliography on all aspects
of civil rights. Books relating to each facet of our civil liberties
are listed. One section is devoted to intergroup relations and organized around such topics as "The Nature of Prejudice," "Intergroup Relations and Human Rights," and "The Negro People:
History, Sociology, Psychology." There is also a list of audiovisual materials and an excellent selection of appropriate fiction
titles. A very useful bibliography because it is so comprehensive,
but the nonfiction annotations are very brief and only hint at the
contents of each book.

Film Catalog, N.Y. Public Library, Donnell Library Center, 20 W. 53rd
St., New York City. The large collection of 16 millimeter films
which is available for rental from the N.Y. Public Library includes many dealing with integration and related topics. There is
a subject index in the catalog and a short summary of the contents
of each film. The films may be borrowed from the library only by
individuals but the catalog lists the primary rental sources which
can be contacted by schools. Catalogs of the various distributors
and more detailed film evaluations are available at the Donnell
Library.

Journal of Negro History, Association for the Study of Negro Life and
History, Washington, D.C. A scholarly journal which presents ar-
ticles by American historians on all aspects of the history of the
Negro in America.

Nelson, Bernard, ed., *The Negro in American History, A Curriculum
Resource Bulletin for Secondary Schools,* The Public Schools of

the District of Columbia, 1964. A brief but comprehensive summary of the history of the Negro in America which is organized so that all or parts of it can be incorporated into a regular American history course. There is considerable emphasis on Negro individuals who made significant contributions to the making of America, and the role of Negro organizations and publications is also stressed. There are short biographies of important American Negroes, selected bibliographies at the end of each unit and an annotated bibliography. There is also a correlation chart which shows how the material in the Bulletin could be incorporated into other social studies courses.

Southern School News, Southern Educational Reporting Service, Nashville, Tennessee. Recommended by several authorities as the best source of detailed, state-by-state information on school desegregation in the South.

The Williamstown Workshop, *A Program for Improving Bill of Rights Teaching in High Schools,* Civil Liberties Educational Foundation, Inc., 200 Park Ave., S., N.Y., 1962. A superb aid for teaching all aspects of individual rights. The authors, a group of high school and college teachers, explain why they feel that the teaching about the Bill of Rights in American secondary schools needs vast improvement and then offer a great variety of meaningful suggestions. For example, they list significant documents which can be incorporated into the teaching of American history and explain the substance and appropriate use of each document which they recommend.

The section "On Equal Education," which begins on p. 93, is a many-faceted lesson plan covering all aspects of the problem. Discussion and research questions are suggested, important Supreme Court cases are summarized, and relevant films for classroom use are described.

RECORDS FOR ALL AGES

FOLKWAYS RECORDS

FC 7406   *Follow the Sunset* with Charity Bailey—folk songs around the world.

FC 7752   *The Glory of Negro History,* written and narrated by Langston Hughes with actual voices of Ralph Bunche and Mary McLeod Bethune.

FC 7114   *An Anthology of Negro Poetry for Young People* compiled and well read by Arna Bontemps.

FC 7312   *The Story of Jazz,* narrated by Langston Hughes.

FC 7402   *Who Built America,* sung by Bill Bonyun—American history through folk songs.

FC 7770   *Snoopycat,* the adventures of Marian Anderson's cat narrated and sung by her.

FC 7533   *Negro Folk Songs for Young People,* sung by Leadbelly, founder of American folk singers.

FC 7431   *The World of Man, Vol. I, His Work,* a story and narration by Harold Courlander.

FA 2187   *Ballads of the Civil War (North)* sung by Hermes Nye.

FA 2188   *Ballads of the Civil War (South)* sung by Hermes Nye.

OTHER LANDS

FC 7262   *There's a Brown Boy in the Ring* by Lord Invader; other children's Calypso songs included.

FC 7110   *Ashanti Folk Tales from Ghana* narrated by Harold Courlander (refers to stories in book by same title).

CIVIL RIGHTS

FH 5590   *The Nashville Sit-in Story* by Guy Carawan.

FH 5591   *We Shall Overcome,* Pete Seeger's Carnegie Hall Concert of June 8, 1963.

FH 5502   *The Sit-in Story* narrated by Edwin Randall.

DO-IT-YOURSELF SONGBOOKS

Each one of these books offers rich background explanation of songs connected with many phases of Negro life.

We Shall Overcome compiled by Guy & Candie Carawan, 1963, Oak.

The Leadbelly Songbook edited by Moses Asch and Alan Lomax, 1962, Oak.

Soldier Songs & Home Front Ballads of the Civil War compiled and edited by Irwin Silber (1964).

John F. Kennedy and the Negro—12" 1. p. Ebony Bookshop, 1820 S. Michigan Ave., Chicago, Illinois 60616

Guide for Teachers on Contributions of Afro-Americans in the American Culture. Rich resource and bibliographies of teaching suggestions by grade level. Order from: Guide for Teachers, 114–53 207 Street, Cambria Heights, Queens, N.Y. 11411

TEACHING UNITS AND BIBLIOGRAPHIES

About 100 Books: A Gateway to Better Intergroup Understanding, Ann G. Wolfe. Covers books published through 1957–58, and groups them by topics and by ages 5 through 16. 36 pp. American Jewish Committee.

Audiovisual Methods of Teaching, Edgar Dale, 300 pages or so of sources, lists, and suggestions for most effective use of audiovisual materials. Dryden.

Bibliography of Audiovisual Aids for Courses in American Literature, Sister Mary Brian; includes records, tapes, films, and filmstrips to help slow readers enjoy more mature literature. Rich with intergroup education ideas as well as cross-fertilization of English and Social Studies education. National Council of Teachers of English.

Books About Negro Life for Children, Augusta Baker, 1961. 21 pages of carefully annotated and recommended books for elementary- and middle-school children. New York Public Library.

Books for Friendship, M. E. Whirter. More than 1000 titles, including songs and games. 94 pages. American Friends Service Committee.

Books for Junior High School, over 900 titles, Philadelphia Fellowship Commission.

Books for Senior High School, over 900 titles, Philadelphia Fellowship Commission.

Educators Guide to Free Films, Educators Progress Service.

Educational Film Guide, H. W. Wilson Company.

Free and Inexpensive Learning Materials. 3000 items listed and classified. 181 pp. George Peabody College for Teachers.

Freedom Pamphlets, Anti-Defamation League of B'nai B'rith.

Freedom Books, Collier Books.

Guide for Teachers on Contributions of Afro-Americans in the American Culture. Grades K–6. By grade level rich resource and teaching suggestions. Order from: Guide for Teachers, 114-53 207 Street, Cambria Heights, Queens, N.Y.

How Series, The. Excellent small books using multi-ethnic illustrations and appealing text for young students. Benefic Press.

How to Utilize Community Resources, National Education Association —National Council for the Social Studies, How to Do It—Series #13.

I Can Hear It Now, albums, and records narrated by Edwin R. Murrow. The first series dramatizes crucial events in history such as the signing of the Magna Charta and the Battle of Gettysburg. Some of them reproduce crucial historical episodes in the twentieth century, while others are devoted entirely to the speeches of outstanding world figures such as Winston Churchill and Franklin D. Roosevelt. Columbia Records.

One Nation Library Series, Anti-Defamation League of B'nai B'rith. Books by Courlander, Douglas, Handlin, Kennedy, Montagu, and Van Til.

Reading Ladders for Human Relations, Heaton and Lewis. 657 books listed and annotated; includes family life, growing up, group membership, socioeconomic differences, and adjusting to new situations. 215 pp. American Council on Education.

Sample Units for New Emphases in Elementary Social Studies. Over 20 sample units graded K–6, for elementary schools. Emphases on Intergroup and Intercultural Education. Written and edited by Elizabeth S. Wright, Assistant Superintendent Bucks County Schools. Address: Office of Education, Bucks County Public Schools, 50 North Main Street, Doylestown, Pennsylvania.

Secondary Resource Units, Education for Social Competence, Quillen and Hanna, Scott Foresman and Co.

Social Understanding Through Literature, Carlsen and Alm, 1954; includes 475 books suitable for secondary school-age students concerning social-political problems. National Council for the Social Studies.

Stories to Remember, a series of this country's democratic heritage, and *These Great Americans,* fifteen-minute biographies of national heroes and heroines. Institute for Democratic Education.

Urban Education Studies, Betty Atwell Wright; Topics range from "A City Is . . ." to "Recreation Is . . ." Large picture albums with 12 prints each. Teachers Guide for usage suggestions, discussion, and supplementary activities. 24-photograph albums also available on individual large cities. New York, The John Day Company, Inc.

World Friends—Picture Albums, Around the World Picture Books, and the "This Is" Series. New York, Friendship Press.

SOURCE INFORMATION

It is impossible to list here all of the sources to which one might send for materials. However, whenever a company or association has been named in earlier references, every effort has been made to include it here. The group or school staff that becomes interested in building up an intergroup education library or resource file will find many other sources and materials, especially as time goes on.

ABINGDON PRESS
810 Broadway
Nashville, Tenn.

ADDISON-WESLEY PUBLISHING CO.
Reading, Mass.

ALBERT M. GREENFIELD
Center for Human Relations
University of Pennsylvania
3935 Locust Street
Philadelphia, Pa.

AMERICAN ASSOCIATION FOR THE UNITED NATIONS
345 East 46th Street
New York City, N.Y.

AMERICAN CIVIL LIBERTIES UNION
170 Fifth Avenue
New York 11, N.Y.

AMERICAN COUNCIL ON EDUCATION
1785 Massachusetts Ave., N.W.
Washington, D.C.

AMERICAN FEDERATION OF LABOR AND CONGRESS OF
    INDUSTRIAL ORGANIZATIONS (AFL–CIO)
Film Division, Department of Education
815 Sixteenth St., N.W.
Washington 6, D.C.

AMERICAN FRIENDS SERVICE COMMITTEE
Suite 220
2 West 20th Street
New York 11, N.Y.

AMERICAN JEWISH COMMITTEE
165 East 56th Street
New York City, N.Y.

AMERICAN JEWISH CONGRESS
15 East 84th Street
New York City, N.Y.

ANCHOR BOOKS
Doubleday and Co.
575 Madison Ave.
New York 22, N.Y.

AMERICAN COUNCIL ON EDUCATION
1785 Massachusetts Ave., N.W.
Washington, D.C.

AMERICAN RED CROSS
703 Whitney Ave.
New Haven, Conn.

ANTI-DEFAMATION LEAGUE OF B'NAI B'RITH
315 Lexington Avenue
New York City, N.Y.   10016

ASSOCIATION FILMS
Broad at Elm Street
Ridgefield, N.J.

ASSOCIATION FOR THE STUDY OF NEGRO LIFE AND
    HISTORY
1538 Ninth Street, N.W.
Washington, D.C.

ASSOCIATION FOR SUPERVISION AND CURRICULUM
    DEVELOPMENT
A Department of the National Education Association (NEA)
1201 Sixteenth Street, N.W.
Washington, D.C.   20036

BANK STREET READERS
McMillan Publishing Co.
Riverside, N.J.

BEGINNER BOOKS, A DIVISION OF RANDOM HOUSE
457 Madison Avenue
New York 22, N.Y.

BENEFIC PRESS
1900 N. Naragansett Ave.
Chicago 7, Ill.

BOBBS-MERRILL CO., INC.
4300 W. 62nd Street
Indianapolis, Indiana   46206

BROADCASTING AND FILM COMMISSION
National Council of the Churches of Christ in the U.S.A.
220 Fifth Avenue
New York 1, N.Y.

BROOKINGS INSTITUTION
1775 Massachusetts Ave., N.W.
Washington, D.C.   20036

CAPITAL PRESS COMPANY
1006 National Press Bldg.
Washington 4, D.C.

CARNEGIE ENDOWMENT FOR INTERNATIONAL PEACE
United Nations Plaza at 46th Street
New York City, N.Y.

CHAMBER OF COMMERCE OF THE UNITED STATES
1615 H Street, N.W.
Washington, D.C.

CHANDLER PUBLISHING COMPANY
San Francisco, Cal.

CHILTON BOOKS—DIVISION OF CHILTON CO.
525 Locust St.
Philadelphia, Pa.   19106

CITIZENSHIP EDUCATION PROJECT
Teachers College
Columbia University
New York City, N.Y.   10027

CIVIC EDUCATION CENTER
Tufts University
Medford, Mass.

COLLIER BOOKS
60 Fifth Avenue
New York City, N.Y.   10011

COLUMBIA UNIVERSITY PRESS
2960 Broadway
New York City, N.Y.   10027

COMMITTEE FOR ECONOMIC DEVELOPMENT
711 Fifth Avenue
New York City, N.Y.

COMMITTEE ON RACE RELATIONS
PHILADELPHIA YEARLY MEETING OF THE RELIGIOUS
     SOCIETY OF FRIENDS
160 North 15th Street
Philadelphia 2, Pa.

COMMONWEALTH OF PUERTO RICO
Migration Division, Department of Labor
322 West 45th Street
New York 36, N.Y.

COMMUNITIES TENSION CENTER
Springfield College
Springfield, Mass.

CONTEMPORARY FILMS
267 West 25th Street
New York 1, N.Y.

CORONET FILMS
Coronet Building
Chicago 11, Ill.

THOMAS Y. CROWELL CO.
201 Park Avenue South
New York, N.Y.   10003

CROWN PUBLISHING CO.
419 Park Avenue
New York, N.Y.   10016

COUNCIL OF STATE GOVERNMENTS
1313 East 60th Street
Chicago, Ill.

THE JOHN DAY COMPANY, INC.
62 West 45th Street
New York, N.Y.   10036

DEPARTMENT OF PUBLIC INSTRUCTION
(Check your own State Education Department)

DEPARTMENT OF PUBLIC WELFARE
(Check your own State and local departments)

DODD, MEAD & COMPANY
432 Fourth Ave.
New York, N.Y.   10016

DOUBLEDAY & CO., INC.
Garden City
Long Island
New York

E. P. DUTTON & CO., INC.
201 Park Ave. S.
New York, N.Y.   10003

EBONY
1820 South Michigan Ave.
Chicago, Ill.   60616

EDUCATIONAL FILM GUIDE
H. W. Wilson Co.
950 University Ave.
New York 52, N.Y.

EDUCATIONAL RECORD SALES
153 Chambers St.
New York, N.Y.

EDUCATORS PROGRESS SERVICE
Randolph, Wisconsin

ENCYCLOPAEDIA BRITANNICA FILMS
1150 Wilmette Ave.
Wilmette, Ill.

FOLKWAYS RECORDS
Service Corporation
165 West 46th Street
New York 36, N.Y.

FOLLETT PUBLISHING CO.
1010 Washington Blvd.
Chicago, Ill.   60607

FREEDOMWAYS
799 Broadway
New York 3, N.Y.

FREE LIBRARY OF PHILADELPHIA
Educational Films Department
Logan Square
Philadelphia 3, Pa. (check your nearest large library)

FREE PRESS OF GLENCOE, INC.
640 Fifth Ave.
New York, N.Y.   10019

FRIENDLY HOUSE PUBLISHERS
65 Suffolk St.
New York, N.Y.

FRIENDSHIP PRESS
475 Riverside Drive
New York, N.Y.   10027

GUIDE FOR TEACHERS (Afro-American History)
114-53 207th Street
Cambria Heights, Queens
New York, N.Y.   11411

GEORGE PEABODY COLLEGE FOR TEACHERS
Division of Surveys and Field Services
Nashville 5, Tenn.

GROLIER INCORPORATED
575 Lexington Ave.
New York, N.Y.   10022

HARCOURT, BRACE & WORLD, INC.
757 Third Ave.
New York, N.Y.   10017

HARPER & ROW, PUBLISHERS
49 E. 33 St.
New York, N.Y.   10016

HARMON FOUNDATION INC.
Division of Visual Experiment
140 Nassau Street
New York 38, N.Y.

HARVARD UNIVERSITY PRESS
79 Garden St.
Cambridge, Mass.   02138

HOLMES BOOK AGENCY
91 Beaufort Place
New Rochelle, N.Y.

HOUGHTON MIFFLIN CO.
2 Park Street
Boston, Mass.   02107

HUMAN RELATIONS COMMISSION
(Check your own local and state organizations)

INTERNATIONAL FILM BUREAU
57 East Jackson Blvd.
Chicago 4, Ill.

INSTITUTE FOR DEMOCRATIC EDUCATION
515 Madison Avenue
New York 22, N.Y.

INSTITUTE OF PACIFIC RELATIONS
129 East 52nd St.
New York, N.Y.

JAM HANDY FILM ORGANIZATION
2821 East Grand Blvd.
Detroit 11, Michigan

JEWISH COMMUNITY RELATIONS COUNCIL
(Check your local and state organizations)

JEWISH LABOR COMMITTEE
25 East 78th Street
New York 21, N.Y.

JOURNAL OF NEGRO EDUCATION
Bureau of Educational Research
Howard University Press
Washington 1, D.C.

ALFRED A. KNOPF, INC.
501 Madison Ave.
New York, N.Y.   10022

J. B. LIPPINCOTT CO.
East Washington Square
Philadelphia, Pa.   19105

LONGMANS, GREEN, AND COMPANY
Apply to David McKay Co.
750 Third Ave.
New York, N.Y.   10017

LOTHROP, LEE & SHEPHARD CO.
419 Park Ave. South
New York, N.Y.   10016

MCGRAW-IIILL BOOK COMPANY
330 W. 42 St.
New York, N.Y.   10036

THE MACMILLAN COMPANY
60 Fifth Ave.
New York, N.Y.   10011

MEDICAL BOOKS FOR CHILDREN
Minneapolis, Minn.

JULIAN MESSNER, INC.
8 West 40th St.
New York, N.Y.   10018

MORROW JUNIOR BOOKS
William Morrow & Co., Inc.
386 Park Ave. South
New York, N.Y.   10016

NATIONAL ASSOCIATION FOR THE ADVANCEMENT OF
   COLORED PEOPLE (NAACP)
20 West 40th Street
New York 18, N.Y.

NATIONAL ASSOCIATION OF MANUFACTURERS
Education Department
14 West 49th Street
New York, N.Y.

NATIONAL ASSOCIATION FOR ELEMENTARY SCHOOL
  PRINCIPALS
A Department of the National Education Association
1201 Sixteenth St. N.W.
Washington, D.C.

NATIONAL ASSOCIATION OF SECONDARY SCHOOL
  PRINCIPALS
A Department of the National Education Association
1201 Sixteenth St. N.W.
Washington, D.C.

NATIONAL BROADCASTING COMPANY, NBC-RCA
Radio Recordings
Radio City
New York, N.Y.

NATIONAL CONFERENCE OF CHRISTIANS AND JEWS
43 West 57th Street
New York 19, N.Y.

NATIONAL COUNCIL FOR THE SOCIAL STUDIES
A Department of the National Education Association
1201 Sixteenth St. N.W.
Washington, D.C.

NATIONAL COMMUNITY RELATIONS ADVISORY COUNCIL
55 West 42nd Street
New York, N.Y.

NATIONAL MUNICIPAL LEAGUE
47 East 68th Street
New York, N.Y.

NATIONAL PLANNING ASSOCIATION
1606 New Hampshire Ave. N.W.
Washington, D.C.

NATIONAL RECREATION ASSOCIATION
8 West Eighth Street
New York, N.Y.

NATIONAL STUDY OF SECONDARY SCHOOL EVALUATION
Washington 6, D.C.

NATIONAL URBAN LEAGUE
14 East 48th Street
New York, N.Y.

NEW YORK PUBLIC LIBRARY
Public Relations Department
5th Ave. and 42nd Street
New York 19, N.Y.

NEGRO HERITAGE
P.O. Box 8153
Chicago, Ill.   60680

PAN AMERICAN UNION PUBLICITY AND DISTRIBUTION
   DIVISION
19th Street and Constitution Ave. N.W.
Washington, D.C.

PANTHEON BOOKS, INC.
22 E. 51 St.
New York, N.Y.   10022

PENGUIN BOOKS, INC.
3300 Clipper Mill Rd.
Baltimore, Md.   21211

PHILADELPHIA FELLOWSHIP COMMISSION
Community Services Department
260 South 15th Street
Philadelphia 2, Pa.

PRENTICE-HALL INC.
Englewood Cliffs, N.J.   07632

PUBLIC AFFAIRS COMMITTEE
22 East 38th Street
New York, N.Y.

PUBLIC AFFAIRS PRESS
419 New Jersey Ave. S.E.
Washington, D.C.   20003

G. P. PUTNAM'S SONS
200 Madison Avenue
New York, N.Y.   10016

RANDOM HOUSE, INC.
457 Madison Avenue
New York, N.Y.   10022

RCA VICTOR
Education Services
Camden, N.Y.

SAVE THE CHILDREN
Box 120
New York 17, N.Y.

SCIENCE RESEARCH ASSOCIATES
259 East Erie Street
Chicago, Ill.   60611

SCOTT, FORESMAN AND COMPANY
433 E. Erie St.
Chicago, Ill.   60611

SILVER BURDETT COMPANY
Park Ave. & Columbia Rd.
Morristown, N.J.

STATE COMMISSION ON HUMAN RIGHTS
(Check your State Commission)

TEACHING FILM CUSTODIANS
25 West 43rd Street
New York 63, New York

UNESCO PUBLICATION CENTER
317 East 34th Street
New York, N.Y.

UNITED ARTISTS ASSOCIATED
247 Park Avenue
New York 17, N.Y.

UNIVERSITY OF CALIFORNIA EXTENSION
Educational Film Sales Department
Los Angeles 24, California

UNIVERSITY OF CHICAGO PRESS
5750 Ellis Ave.
Chicago, Ill.   60637

U.S. COMMITTEE FOR UNICEF
331 East 38th Street
New York City, N.Y.

U.S. DEPARTMENT OF HEALTH, EDUCATION, AND
    WELFARE
Office of Education
Washington, D.C.

U.S. GOVERNMENT
All lists from Sup't. of Documents
U.S. Government Printing Office
Washington, D.C.   20402

UNITED STEELWORKERS OF AMERICA
National Headquarters
Washington, D.C.

UNITED WORLD FILMS
1445 Park Avenue
New York 29, N.Y.

VANGUARD PRESS INC.
424 Madison Avenue
New York, N.Y.   10017

VIKING PRESS
625 Madison Ave.
New York, N.Y.   10022

D. VAN NOSTRAND CO., INC.
120 Alexander Street
Princeton, N.J.   08541

WATTS, FRANKLIN INC.
A Division of Grolier, Inc.
575 Lexington Ave.
New York, N.Y.   10022

HENRY WALCK CO.
19 Union Square West
New York, N.Y.   10003

WESLEYAN UNIVERSITY PRESS
Education Center
Columbus 16, Ohio

WHITTLESEY HOUSE
Division of McGraw Hill Book Co.
330 West 42nd St.
New York 18, N.Y.

WORLD AFFAIRS CENTER FOR THE U.S.
United Nations Plaza at 47th Street
New York City, N.Y.

YALE UNIVERSITY PRESS
149 York St.
New Haven, Conn.

ZENITH BOOKS
Doubleday
Garden City, L.I., N.Y.

INDEX

A

Abrahamson, David A., 25
ACEI. *See* Association for Childhood Education International
Administrators, school, 18, 53, 54, 62, 63, 80, 88ff., 96–97, 102, 162
Adolescence, 35, 68, 113
Adult education, 20, 61, 148
Africans, 121
Alabama, 43
Alaska, 137
Alcoholism, 35, 144
Allport, Gordon W., 65, 71
American Association of Colleges for Teacher Education, 31
American Association of School Administrators, 87
American Council on Education, 87–88, 99fn., 133, 157fn., 158fn.
American Educational Research Association, 87
American Institute of Public Opinion (Gallup Poll), 69

American Protective Association, 140
American Teachers Association, 86
Anthropology, 62, 92, 117
Anti-Defamation League (B'nai Brith), 90, 109fn., 122, 147
Anti-Semitism, 71, 72, 102, 139, 177–178
Army Information and Education Division, 76–77
ASCD. *See* Association for Supervision and Curriculum Development
Association for Childhood Education International (ACEI), 24fn., 26
Association for Supervision and Curriculum Development (ASCD), 24fn., 26fn., 68fn., 87
Attitudes, 37, 62ff., 67ff., 72, 73, 77ff., 83–84, 89, 92–94, 97–99, 101ff., 106ff., 111, 116–117, 128, 163